An Imperfec Storm

By

Kevin Haugh

www.otb.ie

An Imperfect Storm
By Kevin Haugh

Published by:
Outside The Box Learning Resources Ltd.
W6W Tougher's Business Park
Newhall, Naas, Co. Kildare
Tel: 045 409322 (Int: +353 45409322)
Fax: 045 409959 (Int: +353 45409959)
Email: info@otb.ie
Website: www.otb.ie

ISBN: 9781906926366

Edited by: Trióna Marren O'Grady, BA H.Dip Ed. [www.pangurban.ie]

Digitally Printed in Republic of Ireland

Cover Photo (by Mary Haugh): Kevin and Buddy on the White Strand also known as Haugh's Strand in the West Clare Peninsula with the River Shannon on the background and Beale Beach on the Kerry Coastline across the river.

Price: €14.95/£12.95/US$17.95

To Mary, Brian, Ronan - and Buddy

Kindest Regards
& best wishes

— Kevin
18/10/2015

Author Biography:

Kevin Haugh is a cancer survivor, the latest victory in his long list of activities and achievements.

He is a retired Principal of Galvone NS in Limerick City since 2010. From September 2005 to August 2009, a period covered in the book, he held the post of Assistant National Co-ordinator on secondment to Leadership Development for Schools. He has presented papers at numerous conferences and has had education research papers published in Ireland, Europe and New Zealand.

Among his pending publications with OTB Publications are:
- Towards Understanding & Combatting Educational Disadvantage
- Understanding Ireland from Primeval Times to the Flight of the Earls 1607

Nowadays, Kevin and Buddy can be seen strolling around Monaleen, or relaxing by the sea at Haugh's Strand in the West Clare Peninsula, enjoying life as it comes.

My wife Mary with Buddy in Haugh's Strand
with Kilcredaun in the background.

The **Mid-Western Cancer Foundation** was founded by Professor R. K. Gupta, Consultant Medical Oncologist and Director of Cancer Services at the Mid-Western Regional Hospital, Limerick. The foundation works to streamline donations and provide holistic care for patients with Cancer in the Mid-West region, in addition to ongoing research support.

All author royalty proceeds of **An Imperfect Storm** will go directly to the **Mid-Western Cancer Foundation** to support the invaluable services it provides for those diagnosed with cancer and their families. To find out more, visit www.mwcf.ie.

Foreword

In '**An Imperfect Storm**', Kevin Haugh's prose offers us an incredible insight into an upbringing in the West of Ireland, schooling and the teaching profession, the meaning of family and the disruption, over a number of years, caused by an otherwise innocuous lump, first noticed in 2004.

This book, Dr. Haugh's first, is a raw reflection of life, including the interference of the medical profession. It reveals aspects of our existence that many of us, including those who work in the health service, are unaware of, despite the unique patient-doctor relationship. But then, subconsciously, it is perhaps why we strive to help patients to continuing living - the period between birth and death.

The coming into being of this book is apparently my fault, as I had suggested to Dr. Haugh that he should keep a diary, and he did. Best described as an autobiography, '**An Imperfect Storm**' is a wonderful narration in which undoubtedly, all readers will find common themes. It is about life, family and work, and not only about cancer.

There was more apprehension in the writing of this foreword than was involved in clinical decision making with Kevin. However, if nothing else, Kevin's brave, lyrical and at times humorous novel will remind us all that life really is for living.

Rajnish K. Gupta

August 2013

Editor's Note

It was an honour for me to edit this book and I am humbled to have been a part of the process that has brought it to you.

Kevin tells a story that is not unfamiliar to us, but what *is* unique to his story is the insight and the colour with which he tells it. You feel pain when he does. His despair and his hope become yours. You listen to the birds singing and the waves breaking with him. Above all, you become his travelling companion on this voyage of uncertainty.

There is an underlying musicality to Kevin's writing that is soothing and sweet. When I first read it, I was struck by the flow of his story and the unrelenting passion with which he told it. Kevin is a natural story-teller. It was my job to transpose that story into its rightful and permanent glory on the written page.

The voice is Kevin's – I have left that in its purest form. The story is Kevin's and that of his family and friends. The experience he brings to life for us could be anyone's – cancer doesn't care who you are, what you do, or how good your diet is. Cancer is far more than a physical disease – it invades your life and your relationships, and it changes everything you thought you knew.

Kevin's story delivers fear, hope, determination and a very large measure of love and support. I found it to be of great benefit to me in my life, and I'm very sure you will too.

Trióna Marren O'Grady, BA H.Dip Ed.
www.pangurban.ie

CHAPTER ONE

My Past Perfect

"I've never seen a sight that didn't look better looking back."

- *(Wand'rin' Star* sung by Lee Marvin (1970) originally written by Alan J. Lerner (lyrics) and Frederick Loewe (music) for the stage musical *Paint Your Wagon* in (1951)

Home for me was Lisheencrona in the West Clare Peninsula on 1st February, 1954 where I grew up on a farm in a picturesque location overlooking the Shannon Estuary. There was a beach at the end of our land that was often referred to as the White Strand or Haugh's Strand. This beach was my favourite place. Opposite this shoreline on the Kerry coast was Knocknure and the Cliffs of Dooneen, made famous by the Irish ballad of the same name. Haugh's Strand was the utopia of my childhood. I spent my spare time on the beach watching the migratory birds as one season evolved into the next. The haunting cry of the curlew and the seagull in the fading light at wintertime was in stark contrast to when the graceful swallow came speeding to our shores in springtime and glided downwards towards me, bearing its message that summer was nigh.

This was the perfect place to observe the wildlife featured in Gerrit Van Gelderen and Éamonn De Buitléir's RTÉ programme at the time called *Amuigh Faoin Spéir*, and I supplemented it with books on the natural and unspoiled wonders of my world. Consequently, I considered myself something of an authority in the field. I believed I knew the name of every creature, big and small. My knowledge was embellished by the information I gathered from people in the community, especially those in their twilight years. They always had the time and interest to share what they knew. They knew everything about the creatures, even their habits and their secrets - why the seabirds flew in over the peninsula from the Atlantic whenever we were about to get bad weather, why the same birds would fly northwest out to the Atlantic whenever fine weather was imminent, and where each creature spent the winter until the lark soared into the skies to proclaim that spring had arrived. The University of Life had taught them all they shared with me.

Children of my generation were regaled with stories of people who had magic powers, and to upset them was to put yourself in peril. There was the dreaded cry of the Banshee, a fairy woman who could be heard crying under cloak of darkness whenever someone in a local family was about to die. There were also the influential and powerful "little folk", or fairies, who still inhabited the ring or fairy forts. We were told that we would have bad luck if we crossed their paths or disturbed them in any way. Such misfortunes would come in the form of personal injury or sickness that would quicken progress to an early grave. One might also be captured by the fairies and taken to a land of torture from which there was no return.

The fairies had slightly taller friends called leprechauns who were supposed to frequent the wooded areas close to fairy forts. Leprechauns were much less threatening than fairies. In fact, we were told that if we managed to catch one of these little men and stare into his eyes without blinking for five minutes, that they would give us a pot of gold. But there was the dilemma - how could you capture a leprechaun without disturbing the fairies?

My fascination with the world beyond the horizon at that time was stimulated by my interest in stamp collecting. The stamp collecting was a twofold project. There was the constant belief that I would somehow lay my hands on the missing Penny Black, and there was the added curiosity about parts of the world like Sierra Leone, South Africa and the Philippines – some of the exotic places where people from the community worked in the missions as nuns, priests and Christian Brothers. I managed to befriend some of the families of these missionaries, and then I would get the stamps off the letters whenever they wrote home from the mission fields. These interests fed my curiosity regarding the world beyond my childhood horizons and nourished ambition for my maritime future. On one occasion, my interest in stamp collecting was misconstrued as a potential interest in becoming a missionary. I swiftly managed to clarify my position - I had no interest in the clerical life and my curiosity in faraway places formed part of my apprenticeship for wild adventures on the high seas. In as much as I saw it, the world was waiting for me and I was girding myself mentally and physically with the greatest of self-confidence for the challenges that awaited me. The world was my oyster and of that I was certain. My brave talk and bold ambitions were fuelled by my widescreen imagination.

The cargo boats that passed the shoreline planted my fertile imagination with plenty of material regarding the interesting places those boats might have visited. I promised myself that I would be a sailor when I grew up, and visit exotic destinations and sunny climes with sundrenched shores on boats like these. Somewhat similar to the sentiments of *The Last Farewell* sung by Roger Whittaker, I believed that I would smell the fragrance of those islands and the heaving waves that brought me unto them.

I believed that every boat had its own stories to tell me, from riding the foamy brine to docking at sun-kissed ports in the Caribbean where the crew would relax in the shade of a coconut tree before journeying onwards. However, life and fate would lay out a different career path for me that would limit my nautical experiences to trips on the Kilimer to Tarbert car ferry. Eventually, we ventured further offshore on family holidays by car ferry to France in 1993 and 1994, after which I decided I'd had enough of travel by sea. On reflection, I imagine that if I had opted for the seafaring life of my childhood dreams, I might not have made it from one of the ports on the River Shannon downstream as far as Loop Head, where the river enters the Atlantic Ocean. Nevertheless, those childhood dreams were magic to me.

A small pair of binoculars enabled me to read the names of the different cargo ships as they sailed past me up and down the Shannon Estuary. I was able to identify the flags they flew and their country of origin from an atlas that showed the flags of the world, thoughts of far-off lands always stirring my mind. I awoke each day with the prospect of finding a treasure chest washed ashore from some ill-fated pirate ship and the excitement it would bring. That fantasy then morphed into a vision of the unbridled opportunities that finding a magic bottle with a genie in it would afford me. Clearly, my earlier innocence became somewhat diluted as my imagination outgrew its boundaries.

It was on Haugh's Strand that I walked during my turbulent adolescent years whenever I needed to fathom out the problems the world threw at me. I can't say that I found the answers to my dilemmas riding on the rolling waves as they raced onto the beach. I did, however, find solace and refuge there from a world that did not understand me.

I went to primary school in Doonaha N.S. and Kilkee B.N.S. before attending Kilrush C.B.S. for my secondary education. I was given the privilege of reading aloud the Irish version of *The Proclamation of the Republic (Forógra na Poblachta)*, also known as the *1916 Proclamation* or *Easter Proclamation* on Easter Monday, 1966, after Mass in Doonaha N.S. to celebrate the 50th anniversary of the Easter Rising in Ireland, which began on 24th April, 1916. Roll on the centenary celebrations in 2016 and maybe Doonaha will have me back!

Mine was one of the first generations to benefit from the Investment in Education Programme in Ireland at Kilrush C.B.S. secondary school. I have great memories of my time in the school, where the staff enabled us to navigate state exams and empowered us to cope with the trials and tribulations of teenage years. The downside of my years in Kilrush C.B.S. was that we tended to be the bridesmaids in a number of Munster Schools' football finals and semi-finals.

When I finished my Leaving Cert Examination in 1973, I went to work in the underworld in New York - building a sewer disposal unit - until I returned at the end of the summer to attend Marino Training College for primary teachers.

Subsequent to my brief experience in the construction industry in New York, I claimed that I was one of the men who helped build America. When I finished my teacher training in 1975, I decided to devote some more of my time and talents to the benefit of New York City. On this occasion, I worked very much above ground as a doorman on East 36th Street. There, I had my eyes opened by everything a Manhattan night had to offer. The experience was both a social and a cultural shock to me. How could the streets be so busy right through the night? I was mesmerised by the city that never slept.

When I left Ireland in 1973, New York seemed destined to become my home from home. I felt I was en route to becoming another long-term emigrant; although I presented an outward expression of adventure and anticipation of the New York experience, it broke my heart to leave. I was brave to the outside world, brittle on the inside. Parting with my parents at Shannon Airport was so painful that I still carry an aversion to airports rooted in that experience.

My third level education was in Coláiste Mhuire Marino in Dublin where I took a sabbatical from football for most of my first year until a game between first-year and second-year students prompted me to come out of retirement. During our second year, we won the third division Higher Education Leagues in hurling and football. For some inexplicable reason, I found myself drafted into the hurling squad although I had never played the game previously beyond pucking a sliotar around with a few of the team from time to time. Before very long, I was playing full forward on the hurling team to the dismay of the unsuspecting opposition we met on our route to glory. I can say with absolute certainty that I never played well in the position but I was assured that my unorthodox "left-handed hurling artistry" made life difficult for those playing against us.

It was great to finish the year with two All-Ireland medals. They would be my first and my last, while some of my teammates went on to distinguish themselves at inter-county and all-Ireland levels. However, my own record is unique in that I never played on a losing hurling team. We won all of our games in the Marino colours and that brought down the curtain on my short and unexpected hurling career.

After the summer of 1975 in New York and the distractions it offered, I found it difficult to settle into my teaching career at home in Limerick. There were many times when I thought seriously about packing my bags and heading stateside again until a chance meeting with an ex-girlfriend, Mary Garvey. Cupid had his way, and thoughts of emigrating were supplanted with plans of marriage. Mary and I got married on 30th June, 1979. We had two children subsequently; Brian was born in September, 1983, and Ronan completed our family when he was born in January, 1988.

Mary and I – when we were young! - 1976

I qualified as a primary teacher in 1975 and I began my teaching career in St. Kieran's CBS in Limerick City. The school became a lay-run school in 1986 when the Irish Christian Brothers handed it over to the parish because of declining numbers in their community. I was appointed principal of St. Kieran's Boys National School in 1998. Five years later in 2003, St. Kieran's B.N.S. was amalgamated with the girls' school next-door to us and I became principal of the new school, Galvone N.S.

In retrospect, my experience as a principal in both schools was summed up best by the great Con Houlihan when he described the Dubliners: "The Dubliners were all individualists - Luke and Ronnie and Ciaran and John and Barney were leaves from different trees blown together by the wind..." (Con Houlihan, 1984). In similar manner, the teachers I worked with made up a diverse group of individuals who were already appointed to the staff of the school before I was appointed principal. It goes without saying that there were many opinions and it was my task to unite and lead them towards the one vision. I'm fairly sure we hit at least some of the right notes and managed to stay in harmony in the best interest of the children and the school community.

My life was not singly dedicated to school and academia. In fact it was anything but. I was a reluctant pupil, and to compound matters, I found the discipline of study required for exam preparation torturous because it took me forever to learn what seemed to come naturally to others. To manage my shortcomings, I developed a coping mechanism - remembering by association.

When I began teaching, my late father reminded me that I needed to constantly up-skill to stay abreast with the changes and demands of my chosen profession. He explained if I failed to move with the times in my work, I would be like a farmer who did not embrace change and I would fall behind everyone. He outlined the consequences to me both professionally and personally. He would finish imparting his knowledge of such matters on a wise note: "Life is like a pencil. If you do not keep it sharpened regularly, it will get very blunt with use over time."

During the late seventies and eighties, I taught sixth classes. There was a great shortage of secondary school places in Limerick at the time, and consequently, teachers were judged by the manner in which their pupils were placed in the "magnet schools". It was a crude and cruel form of teacher evaluation. However, nothing lasts forever, and with the passage of time and the decline in the primary school population, eventually the tables turned and post-primary schools began visiting us to attract prospective students. Promotional videos and the promise of computer facilities were the order of the day as they vied for numbers. During this time, a colleague of mine joked that at the rate some schools were promoting themselves, we would very soon have them coming to us at Christmas with a turkey under one arm and a bottle of our favourite vintage under the other.

Having survived the eighties, I did three modules on Effective Management with Open University before doing a Masters in Education Management and a Graduate Diploma in Remedial Education simultaneously, all of which challenged me academically and professionally by engaging me in the processes of Action Research and Self-Evaluation. I was encouraged to take my studies a step further and I enrolled to do a PhD study in the University of Limerick in the summer of 1998, just before I found myself in the position of principal of Galvone N.S. I had never planned to become a principal, but I now decided that I would not be a reluctant one. In hindsight, it was a great decision. I focused my study on education provision and participation in the community from 1975 to 2000 and, based on the findings, I made recommendations for the provision of education in a village model campus with all services under one roof to meet the educational needs of the community in the 21st century. The title of the study was *Towards a New Model of Educational Provision and Participation for an Inner-City Community, in Limerick City, Ireland, 2001.*

With my parents, Jackie and Annie Haugh, 22 Sep 1984.

While I spent my life in the teaching profession, I also chanced my arm at other commercial ventures, some of which were more memorable than others. There were occasions when I found myself in richly diverse part-time roles, such as van driver, rock band manager and nightclub doorman. Working in nightclubs meant that I had to assume the more unlikely roles of peacemaker, negotiator, or stand-in disc jockey whenever the resident DJ felt the need to chat up a girl who caught his eye. The first occasion I obliged, I was given a hurried brief on how the deck operated, which seemed straightforward enough until I was asked to put on *La Bamba* after playing just two or three records. I duly agreed and when the music began, I realised I was playing the records upside-down. Fortunately, the flipside of *La Bamba* was a slow record and the punters did not complain. Some even remarked at the end of the night that they thought it was quite a good move on my part. Little did they know! It was a close call. Things could just as easily have gone calamitously wrong for me while the DJ was away making a favourable impression on the lady who in due course was to become his wife.

In my role as nightclub doorman, I was exposed to the full gamut of patrons' behaviour, from the absolute rudeness of a small element of the yuppie crowd to the affable decorum of the bikers. These people were a remarkable group and will forever hold a warm place in my heart. Their manners made them a people apart for all the right reasons. Close to the bikers was a group that frequented a venue known as the "Hippie Hop" where the music was loud and the people were fabulous. They came for a good time and went home happy, unlike some of the yuppies who defied description for all the wrong reasons when a fit hit them. Some would suggest that my affiliation with the patrons of the "Hippie Hop" was coloured by whatever I inhaled from the secondary smoke at the venue!

CHAPTER TWO

Casting Off – Destination Unknown

"By a high star our course is set. Our end is Life. Put out to sea."

- Louis *MacNeice*

2004 was a momentous year in my life. On 20th January, I had the privilege of welcoming the then President, Mary McAleese, to the school. It was a great honour for me to meet and greet her on behalf of the school community, and her visit was a most memorable occasion.

Ronan celebrated his 16th birthday on 30th January, I reached a half century a few days later on 1st February, our 25th wedding anniversary was on 30th June, and we celebrated Brian's 21st birthday on 22nd September. Life seemed to be good to us and so it was.

I registered for the West Clare Mini-Marathon in November. This event is organised in support of cancer patients in my native West Clare and I felt I wanted to participate. I had been consumed by the "running boom" of the eighties, during which time I ran thirteen marathons. I finished six of these in less than three hours, with a personal best of two hours, forty-nine minutes and thirty-seven seconds in the Cork City Marathon in 1983. It was my first time breaking three hours for the marathon, which until then had been a major ambition of mine.

Running taught me to get the best out of myself both mentally and physically, as I learned to push the body to levels of fitness I never thought possible. My training schedule included track sessions of twenty-four 100-metre time trials with one-minute rest periods, hill training in Cratloe Woods and 10 km time trials on the road, to list some of the sessions we did in training. I believe that the discipline of training gave me the mental steel to push my body in a manner in which I had never done before in my life. It trained me to power myself beyond the pain barrier and keep going when it would have been a lot easier to give up. There was also the ongoing competition between the group members where no quarter was given. I maintain that the self-discipline and mental conditioning I developed in those training sessions served me well in the challenges that were about to unfold. Running was my opium in those days; it lifted the human spirit above the trials and tribulations of everyday life. Running and sport taught me in the best terms possible that nothing comes easy, life is tough and there are times when you have to be even tougher to survive. This philosophy served me well when I adopted it in life, at work and in adversity.

Unaware of what would unfold in the coming two weeks, I focused on a training schedule that would culminate in my running the New York Marathon the following year, November 2005. The timing was perfect. The prospect of visiting NYC and Central Park in autumn during the Halloween break sounded idyllic. This was it; training for the West Clare Mini-Marathon would get me kick started and it would be like the good old days, running once again. I began to look forward to getting the mind and body into shape. Happy days were here again. Even though my body had reached the half-century mark, I was a boy again at heart. The world felt like a wonderful place, and indeed it was. There was so much to look forward to and running would provide me with an escape valve for whatever stresses the day job might throw at me. Once again, I had a plan of action that would serve me well, and at the same time, ensure my wellbeing. This was the perfect situation.

While I was taking a shower after a training run on 4th December, I noticed a slight swelling of the glands on the left side of my neck. Initially, I told myself that it was nothing to worry about. However, I decided as a precaution to show it to our family GP, Dr. Shinkwin, when I had a routine check-up with him on Wednesday, 8th December. He made an appointment for me to be seen by a surgeon the following day. While Dr. Shinkwin did not say anything to alarm me, I was concerned at the urgency with which he wanted an appointment for me. His prompt action then proved lifesaving in the weeks, months and years ahead.

I tried to convince myself that the surgery would be a routine procedure and that nothing sinister would be found. Following the consultation with the surgeon on Friday, 10th December, I was admitted to hospital two days later on Sunday evening and a biopsy was taken the following morning.

Thankfully, I did not suffer any ill effects from the anaesthetic. Others in the hospital ward were very ill and I thanked my lucky stars that everything was going so well for me, so I passed the time reading. Time in hospital goes slowly. I did not complain as I assured myself that I would be out of the place in a day or two and back at work. Night came and went. The usual hospital routines signalled the arrival of the morning of a day that would change the rest of my life.

At 7.50 am on the morning after surgery, I was reading Nelson Mandela's *"Long Walk to Freedom"* when a doctor came to my bedside and said, "I see you have a tumour and there is a problem with your liver", and then he left. Blindsided by his remarks, I was in absolute shock. I had a tumour in my liver. Oh, my God. To the best of my limited knowledge on the matter, it appeared to me that I would die, and very soon too. Thoughts of what would become of my wife Mary, my sons Brian and Ronan, and my mother raced through my head. I was terrified. I was not ready to die. This was not in the script. My mind felt as if it would explode. My whole world was caving in. This could *not* be for real.

When the surgeon came along some time later, I asked him what the outcome was. He told me that he wouldn't have any results from the laboratory for a week and he would see me then. Shortly afterwards, I was discharged. I remember walking out of the hospital and thinking that it was going to be a long week. I also pondered what the future had in store for me. Somehow, I would have to keep up appearances for everybody's sake, although my mind was as ragged as a scarecrow in a storm.

I felt that I had to tell Mary what the doctor had said about a tumour and a problem with my liver. To add to the agony, we would have to wait a week for the results of the biopsy. While we were at our wits end, we decided that there was no point in causing those close to us undue worry. We employed our best efforts to keep up a brave front and convince ourselves that the outcome might be favourable. We even tried to persuade ourselves that it might be some infection I'd picked up swimming in Killaloe with Buddy, the canine member of our family, in one of the lakes all through the autumn when I was trying to build up the muscle mass around his ailing hip. However, no matter how much we tried to make ourselves believe that the gods might look favourably upon us, the signs were ominous like voices in the dark telling us that there was trouble ahead.

I began to keep a diary of events as they happened – the diary from which this book evolved. I found these diaries invaluable in the days, months and years that were to follow. They served as a catharsis and motivation platform in the journey that lay ahead, as I used an inspirational quotation as a heading for each day's entry into what are now called my cancer diaries. The diaries became a wailing wall of sorts to me where I recorded the highs and lows of my journey. There were entries of hope and despair together with rants of anger, often penned in a language and tone that was not the material of lullabies or bedtime reading. I let it rip with the vigour of a demented cuckoo clock. I wrote down exactly what tormented me when I was afraid, angry or upset, and this catharsis enabled me to cope and possibly save those close to me from the brunt of my feelings at a time when all of us were going through an intense emotional experience.

We were blank on the outside, turbulent on the inside. We were hoping for the best from the lab results, and in some manner, trying to brace ourselves for the worst. Finally, on mid-winter's day, Tuesday, 21st December, while the Neolithic enthusiasts enjoyed the winter solstice at Newgrange Stone Age Passage Tomb in Co. Meath, Mary and I were bracing ourselves for the results of the surgeon's biopsy, which we would receive later in the day. As the long shadows of evening stretched in the fading light of the shortest day in the Northern Hemisphere, Mary and I entered the surgeon's office at 3.19 pm. We were informed that I had non-Hodgkin's lymphoma, and that he would refer us to the Cancer Centre in the local Regional Hospital. At the time, I did not know what lymphoma was, not to mention the difference between Hodgkin's lymphoma and non-Hodgkin's lymphoma.

We were devastated. This was our greatest nightmare. My whole world imploded. There was no future. I was overwhelmed with despair, helplessness, anger and hopelessness. The end seemed near and the past seemed irrelevant. It was impossible to come to grips with the fact that I had a malignant tumour removed from my neck and my chances of survival would depend on the findings of further medical tests. The waiting would be painful and the future looked bleak.

I was terrified. The fear was tempered with anger. My prospects did not enthuse me. My lifeline seemed to snap suddenly and contract. I felt I was living my worst nightmare.

We stood on the footpath outside the surgeon's rooms in absolute desperation. A black sea of pain engulfed us. Mary phoned our close friends, Michael and Marie O'Brien, with the bad news. Michael suggested that we contact Dr. Shinkwin, which we did. We entered his surgery, where a large number of patients sat waiting in the waiting room at 4 pm. He was letting out a patient at the time and he insisted on seeing us immediately. He simply stopped the clock, and words fall short in describing the professional and compassionate manner in which he took care of us in our distressed condition. He discussed the diagnosis with us in a helpful and supportive manner, as is his way. I will never forget his kindness and consideration. He is a consummate gentleman and professional.

On our way home that day, we called to Michael and Marie O'Brien before the dreadful ordeal of breaking the news to Brian and Ronan. It was official now, in that our worst fears had been confirmed. The boys were numbed when we told them and sought to cling to every straw of hope. It was all that any of us could do. We were still terrified. I had just been diagnosed with cancer and there was no getting away from it. We were not long home when I got a phone call from the Regional Hospital to say that Professor Gupta, consultant oncologist, would see me the following day. At least we would have more information before the Christmas holidays.

We broke the bad news to our respective families and good friends. I decided that I would not tell my mother until I went to collect her to bring her to our home for Christmas. Our close friends, Richard and Marie Power, called over to us soon after I had spoken to Richard. We had a few drinks and talked late into the night.

The following day, the 22nd December, was the last day of term at school before the Christmas holidays. As my appointment with Professor Gupta was scheduled for later that day, I decided that I would go to work and that I would inform the staff that I had been diagnosed with cancer. It was a very difficult decision to break such news to them on the day of the Christmas Holidays, but I felt it was my duty to tell them in person. Equally, I preferred that they hear an accurate account from me, rather than the exaggerated versions churned out by the rumour mill.

Mary and I went to the Mid-Western Cancer Centre day ward in the Regional Hospital, Dooradoyle, for a noon appointment. The unit is located at the rear of the hospital and we passed the mortuary on the way. A chill ran through me. Finally, we reached the Cancer Centre that would become part of my life for the unforeseeable future. Life was now peppered with uncertainty and both of us were intensely frightened by the prospect of what more today's experience held in store for us. I was angry that I had cancer. I wasn't ready to die and I desperately wanted to live. There were worse obligations than Christmas shopping, I told myself. Take away the cancer and I will never complain about shopping or anything else ever again. I bargained with whatever gods might be prepared to listen to my pleas. But the lights were off and there was nobody home. I shrank in fear.

There was no masking the terror that raced through my veins as we made our way from the car park towards the entrance of the Cancer Centre. The automatic doors opened in front of us and it felt like we were walking into a reception area which would lead us to the waiting room for a living purgatory and eventual death. Although the centre was decorated for Christmas, the festive baubles did nothing to blunt the intolerable truths that are told to cancer patients behind the doors of the consultation rooms. We were about to become part of the world behind those closed doors. The short wait in the reception area was nerve-wracking.

At 12 o'clock, we were taken to a private consultation room that we subsequently referred to as the crying room for our meeting with Professor Gupta and his medical team. We were treated in a most compassionate and professional manner. He gave us all the information they had on my condition. Although I realise now that the long-term prospects at the time were better than what they would have been with most other forms of cancer, that realisation did not ease the pain, shock and reality for me. I was told at that consultation that my cancer could kill me. That was my new reality. I could ignore neither the facts nor the professional opinion that I had cancer and it could kill me. Some start to Christmas. Would I ever see another one? I was afraid to ask anybody else in the fear that I would be told this one was the last.

CHAPTER THREE

Choppy Waters, Sea Mists

"I learned that courage was not the absence of fear, but the triumph over it. The brave man is not he who does not feel afraid, but he who conquers that fear."

- Nelson Mandela

When our consultation was complete, we left the Cancer Centre tearful, terrified and tormented. Any semblance of composure or festive spirit that had remained was vanquished. No matter how hard we tried to be optimistic, the harsh reality of the situation was that the angel of death had sought me out and would haunt our home, day and night. This was a far cry from running the New York City Marathon. The compass of life had now changed direction from thoughts of marathon running to thoughts of which cemetery I'd be buried in and how soon.

I travelled to West Clare on 23rd December to collect my mother and break the news to her. I felt it was best to tell her on a need-to-know basis. I had cancer and I would be commencing treatment in January. I would have further tests and we would find out the direction the treatment would take us. What I did not tell her was that I was told that the cancer could kill me. She was upset enough, and what benefit would such detail have been to her at her stage in life? The news was bad enough for her to cope with, and I would not burden her further. It was a miserable start to her Christmas. The journey back to Limerick with her was filled with questions for which I did not have the answers. My mother turned to prayer for a miracle. Prayer was her armour, especially in times of uncertainty such as this.

We got through Christmas in a haze and tried to keep up appearances for everybody's sake. It was tough going. Fear and uncertainty had gripped us. It was like looking in on our lives from the outside. We decided to make the best of the season, even though the fear was ever-present. Despite our best efforts to put it to the back of our minds, even temporarily, it dogged us day and night. It was a balancing act. We could not hide the reality of the situation that was unfolding and we did not want to worry my mother and the two boys any more, because they were already quite upset. All of us sought hope in the percentages game, because there was a 95% success rate with the treatment that I was about to undertake in January. We did our best to believe that the odds were comfortably stacked in my favour. On reflection, I feel we made the best of the situation and it served to bind us together as a family.

We sent the boys out to enjoy themselves as much as possible in the hope that they might avoid getting bogged down in the gloom that enveloped our home. At the end of the Christmas holidays, I remember Ronan remarking that in the run up to Christmas, he'd wondered if he would be allowed into town over the holidays, and when the news broke about my illness, he felt that it was going to be the worst Christmas ever. In the end, he said, he was almost exhausted from the nightlife because instead of asking for permission to go out, both Mary and I were actually encouraging him to go out. We were happy that the emerging situation did not spoil Christmas completely for the boys. At least going out at night gave them some release from what was unfolding at home.

Unfortunately, there was no such respite for Mary. We cried until we thought our hearts would break. The fear of dying was beyond description. There were times when I felt as if the fear alone would choke me before the cancer had its opportunity to destroy me.

I was angry and devastated that I might not grow old with Mary. I might not see Brian and Ronan grow into adult life. I might not be there to give them fatherly support and enjoy watching them become independent adults. I might not see them find partners in life and if they had children in due course, I might not see my grandchildren and share my twilight years with them, imparting a chest of stories I had stored for them in my heart. I felt robbed and cheated of the dreams that I had shaped in my mind of how I would spend my time when I retired. For me, these emotions were not borne out of a sense of entitlement, rather a relationship with expectation that comes with what might be intuitive progression into my twilight years. It goes without saying that my relationship with expectation was severely dented!

There would be no sunset years for me. Instead, I would come to an abrupt end, execution by cancer. Cancer was my judge and jury. There would be no trial before the hanging. Chemotherapy would at best commute my sentence. The horror stories I had heard of its side effects were daunting. I was concerned for my mother who was now in her eighties. I wanted to be around to take care of her, which up until now, I believed was in keeping with the natural order of things. I worried about what would become of her if I were no longer in a position to do so.

I had a CAT scan, bone marrow test and blood tests on 30th December. The bone marrow biopsy was not a very pleasant experience, as I could hear and feel the instrument grating in my pelvis as it extracted the marrow. But I knew the pain would pass. We got the results of the scan and blood tests on Wednesday, 6th January, which brought some relief to us in that the cancer had not spread to any of my organs. I had follicular lymphoma, which was at stage 3B. Stage 3 means that the lymph nodes on both sides of the diaphragm are involved, and it was classified as B because I had symptoms, which in my case were night sweats. The situation was serious enough, but it could have been worse because cancer is rated in stages from one to four. At least I was in with a chance! I would be going on a course of chemotherapy that had a 95% success rate. Although I was not a gambling man, I had to believe that my chances were good, short-term at least. Every day was a bonus at this juncture. Brian and Ronan were as buoyed as one could be in the circumstances by the positives we took from those results. Both of them said that they slept well that night for the first time since the cancer saga began.

Over the Christmas period, I was in quite an amount of pain because my glands had swollen. Added to that, we had to get up a few times every night and change the bedclothes because I had very heavy night sweats. I couldn't sleep properly because I was in considerable pain, despite taking painkillers and propping myself up with pillows. The pain and sweats were getting progressively worse with each night that passed. I went to the cancer day centre on Tuesday, 11th January with a view to starting my treatment as soon as possible. Professor Gupta and the medical team made arrangements to commence treatment on Thursday, 13th January. There was no room for superstition around starting on the 13th - I just needed to get started and that was it.

Well-meaning people suggested that we should seek second opinions, follow diets, visit faith healers and go on pilgrimages. We respected their good intentions. Mary trawled the internet in search of information on my type of cancer. We all know that some of the information posted on websites is flawed and should be handled with caution, but when one is as desperate as she was, that's easy to forget. However, Professor Gupta pointed her in the direction of reputable websites, and together with the information she garnered from Professor Gupta and the medical team, we made a definite decision not to engage in the alternative medicine routes. The evidence and expertise in favour of conventional medicine were compelling and weighed heavily in favour of that route. We did, however, try to remove as many processed foods from our diet as possible.

The time from diagnosis to the beginning of chemotherapy felt like an eternity because I wanted to start the treatment as soon as possible. To me, it was like fighting a fire. The sooner we started fighting it with chemotherapy, the better the chance we had of bringing it under control and extinguishing it. This attitude might sound crazy, but I believed that any time wasted could mean ground lost in the fight against the enemy. At that stage, if the medical team had asked me to drink petrol and swallow flames, I believe I would have done it, as we put our full faith in them. We were learning to ride the wave now that we were living in times that were more uncertain than we would ever have thought they could be.

CHAPTER FOUR

Lost in Uncharted Waters

"Faith is taking the first step even when you don't see the whole staircase."

- Dr. Martin Luther King

On the morning of Thursday, 13th January, Mary dropped Ronan to school at Ardscoil Rís on the Ennis Road at the other side of the city from where we live. I fell back to sleep until I was called from downstairs by our dog, Buddy. I had to summon all my resources to get out of the bed, dreading the venture into the unknown that was in store for all of us. But I realised that staying in bed wasn't going to make the inevitable go away either. It was time to take a cue from Arthur Miller's *Death of a Salesman*; "Never fight fair with a stranger, boy. You'll never get out of the jungle that way." I had a fight on my hands now with a stranger called cancer. My mind was full of doubts as to whether I had the required strength and courage necessary for the fight with cancer. This was a most fearsome situation. I would have to galvanise myself as best I could and try to meet the challenge head on. That would be easier said than done. Eventually, I got out of bed and made my way downstairs where Buddy joined me for breakfast. Soon Mary arrived back from the school run and we made our way to the Cancer Centre at the Regional Hospital. Conversation was limited as I believe that both of us were consumed by fear and apprehension.

I was absolutely terrified as we entered the day ward, and I think Mary was feeling likewise. It was an eerie experience, like entering the waiting room for death! It was a place where medical endeavour and expertise were sacrificed to my fear and ignorance. I was an uneducated novice. I saw death in the eyes of every patient and I imagined that mine must sooner or later tell the same tale. I felt I had walked up a dead-end street where cancer pillaged and destroyed us before it fed us to Death, the ferryman all the while waiting impatiently to take our souls across the River Styx. Looking at the medical team, I knew that they would do their best to buy each of us as much time as they possibly could, depending on our individual circumstances. I was in an unenviable position beginning my term on the yellow road. Cancer had me on death row.

We were met by Professor Gupta, who gave us the good news that the bone marrow sample taken on 30th December proved to be free from cancer. He again went through the plan of action with us in professional detail while managing to be most supportive and sympathetic towards ourselves and our circumstances. The cancer-free bone marrow would prove vital in the long term, if there was to be a long term. Professor Gupta then gave me an option to have more bone marrow taken for further molecular analysis on a date that I might feel up to having it taken. I jumped at the opportunity and asked him if I could have it done as soon as possible. Procrastination was never my habit, and in the current circumstances, I was not likely to change my ways. Professor Gupta wasted no time and put everything in place to have the procedure done immediately. The bone marrow was taken and on its way for further analysis in less than fifteen minutes.

Once the bone marrow procedure was taken care of, I was prepared for the chemotherapy. I did not know what to expect from it. I hadn't even a notion of how it would be given to me. I took a place at one of the round tables in the day ward at which the procedure would take place. There were facilities to accommodate three patients at each table. The nurse designated to attend to my procedure for the day explained the process to me. I would have blood tests initially and once the results were back, the chemotherapy process would go ahead. It would be infused through a line inserted into a vein in my hand. If, however, the situation with the blood tests was not favourable, the process could not proceed. So it was not a simple case of just turning up and having the treatment. There was a series of procedures to be passed in advance of the infusion of the chemotherapy, which began at 11.45 a.m. and was completed at 5.15 p.m. I also received an infusion of Rituximab, which is a monoclonal antibody. This drug is designed to find a particular type of cancer cell in the body. Its job was to seek and destroy.

When I got home, I felt like a child who had spent his first day at school as I regaled Brian and Ronan with the proceedings of the day until bedtime. Sleep eluded me until after 3 a.m. I was awakened by the mellow tones of a blackbird just before the sky paled in the east for daybreak. After due serenading from the plumed minstrel with his mouth of gold, I got up bright and cheery and on a high with steroids, much to the amusement of everyone at home and especially the staff when I got to school. However, I was advised that the first week after treatment was the "good week", the second week was the week during which one might feel less energy, and by the third week I would be on an upward curve again. I was also told that energy loss is a cumulative process and I would experience a 5% loss of energy with each treatment over the scheduled course of chemotherapy. It beat the alternatives that usually accompany cancer.

The next session was on Wednesday, 2nd February. On this occasion, Brian, who was in college at the time, made what I believe was a very brave decision to accompany me. I don't think I would have had the courage he displayed if I had been in his shoes. Equally, I felt a strong sense of both he and Ronan stepping up to the plate in taking responsibility for matters that I was gradually less able to handle. It was their way of taking care of me, and I really appreciated it.

There was nothing that couldn't be discussed. If questions needed to be asked, they were asked and we tried our best to keep the bright side out. I am sure that there were times in which I failed miserably to live up to my responsibilities and pull my weight. However, Mary, Brian and Ronan never complained about picking up the slack for me.

Again, the procedure began with blood tests. I was examined by the doctor and as soon as the results came back from the laboratory, chemotherapy commenced. The day went more quickly than usual, thanks to Brian's company - we critiqued his final year project. It was a great learning experience for me around the role of non-executive directors in companies. In keeping with our relationship, which I hope was mature, we challenged and respected each other's point of view whenever common ground eluded us. I continued to encourage him to follow his dreams because I believed he had what it took to turn those dreams into reality. I hoped that I would be around to see Brian and Ronan realise their dreams. I was informed on the life expectancy that prevailed around my illness but I would never stop trying to exceed expectations. Somewhere in the recesses of my mind, there was a voice enunciating a phrase from Chemistry lessons in Kilrush C.B.S. that "the exception proves the rule." I hoped that my experience would be the exception that would prove the rule in this instance. I also based my hope on the dictum that hope never abandons you, you abandon it.

It wasn't all doom and gloom. One morning I had a visit at school from a parent who presented in a very distressed state with three offspring in tow. He proceeded to tell me of the trauma suffered by their family and extended families on hearing that I was in hospital the previous week "with the cancer," and how upset they were to hear that I had died at the weekend. He went on to tell me that it would have been a terrible thing for me to die, and it would only make matters worse if he and his family missed the funeral.

This person continued on to say that he and his extended family had held a wake in my honour over the weekend. He assured me that they had drunk copious amounts of alcohol and said several rosaries for the good of my soul. He would turn to his children from time to time and call on them to affirm his story and how they played their part in the wake by saying their own decades of the rosary for me. Whenever he engaged with them to verify their participation, they would begin to whimper until he told them that there was no need to cry because I was not "dead anymore", at which point he would come closer and gave me a good shake to show the children that I was very much alive. I was assured that the family was very relieved to see that I was still alive and looking well because they would have been very disappointed to miss the funeral. He also told me that he and his family would want to take out my remains in a casket and give me a horse-drawn carriage funeral, the kind of funeral a man like me deserved! They would also ensure that I was laid down "properly" in my grave where they would bid me their last farewells before serenading me with a few bars of *The Fair of Spancill Hill,* because they had met me many a time at horse fairs I used to frequent with my brother-in-law Pat O'Neill, and it was at those fairs that they really got to know me.

To bring proceedings to a close, he informed me several times that I would have been a terrible loss and then turned to his children who would repeat the words "terrible loss, terrible loss" in a chorus of agreement with him. Eventually, when it seemed that he was just about running out of compliments for me, he produced a document from an inside pocket and placed it on my desk for immediate signing. He told me to sign it quickly because if I had died, there would have been nobody to sign the form and junior wouldn't have any suit for Confirmation. Once I had the form signed, he assured me of a good wake and a decent burial in due course. Then he took his leave. I was left to ponder the ceremony with which I might be taken to my final resting place. Surely it would be an event not to be missed.

The weeks passed, and before very long the cumulative effect of the medication began to take its toll. There were good days and days that were not so good. My taste buds were affected by the chemotherapy. My energy levels fluctuated. There were extremes from constipation to diarrhoea. Bouts of nausea, abdominal pain, blinding headaches, blurred vision, difficulty concentrating and the cumulative effect of the chemotherapy made it feel like I was living with a permanent hangover, only this time it was without the enjoyment of the night before. These experiences were compounded by the ever-present night sweats and a foul body odour during the day, which necessitated extra attention to personal hygiene, lashings of aftershave, body lotion and deodorant.

Three Rules of Work: 1. Out of clutter, find simplicity. 2. From discord, find harmony. 3. In the middle of difficulty lies opportunity.

-   Albert Einstein

Life had to go on and there were times when my working day proved a welcome distraction in that it kept me from imploding and brooding. Professor Gupta encouraged me to work if I felt up to it. Work proved helpful in keeping as much routine and normality in my life as possible, and for this I was very grateful. In retrospect, I know that I never welcomed the sound of my morning alarm for two reasons; I was never a dawn person, and secondly, with each passing day, my poor body struggled more to get out of bed as the cumulative effects of the chemotherapy hit home.

However, once I got going and shook off the morning's aches and grumbles, it was good to be alive and on the frontline. The school was a vibrant place. I could be assured of regular uplifts when staff endeavours bore fruit as children blossomed and flourished both socially and academically. One outcome of the pupil-staff synergy was acknowledged at this time when the school was awarded one of the Make it Happen Awards with a bursary of €600 and a winner's plaque for the Social and Education Initiative we had in the school. We were in the winners' enclosure and had cause for celebration, together with the affirmation that we were doing something laudable. Everyone enjoys times like this.

I realised that the demands of my job were a blessing in disguise. It gave me reason to get up and get out every morning to meet whatever challenges the day brought. However, nobody's job is perfect and mine was no exception. There were times when I would have been delighted if some of those challenges, like dealing with discipline issues, fractious staff relations and the burgeoning pile of paperwork had disappeared into thin air. I also had to maintain a high profile and affirm those who were doing a good job. One of the less desirable responsibilities of the job was to take appropriate action if underperformance or something untoward was germinating in any quarter. However, there were other challenges that compensated for that. I was constantly learning in my role as school principal, and focused on keeping a clear mind on my work. I was aware of the great people in the school team and gave them professional support and affirmation. I drew on the collective wisdom of the partners in the school community - pupils, parents, teachers and all other members of staff - and concentrated on keeping the leadership compass pointed in the right direction to meet the emerging needs of the school in a rapidly changing and challenging environment. It was a case of what some leadership aficionado referred to as keeping the herd grazing in the same direction.

In the absence of good leadership people will follow anyone and in the absence of all leadership people will do as they please.
-   Unknown

The greatest challenge of leading a team always comes from the negative cultures that exist in the workplace. I found that despite my then circumstances, there was no exception to the rule. All would have their roles, like the negaholic, to whom nothing is possible, and each believes that they know best from experience; how they have seen everybody but themselves getting it all wrong. They garner support from the saboteur whose purpose is to undermine and sabotage by all means at their disposal. Their resourcefulness when put to the task is remarkable. They seem to feel honour-bound to challenge every decision and bear unending animosity towards anybody in a position senior to them. Then there is the "keeper of the nightmare" who revels in regaling their audience about the time that the last new initiative failed so badly despite their original warnings that it was never going to succeed, or in sport where they excel in recalling when you had a bad game or missed an easy opportunity to win the match.

The prima donnas, or attention seekers, are those who choose to portray themselves as the people who do everything for the club or the school. They can fool you into believing that the sun would not rise in the morning if they did not make it happen. They would tell you that they carried the team/school on their backs for years. Legends in their own minds! Most places have the poor martyr who is never appreciated; gets all the tough jobs that nobody else would manage and without ever a word of thanks for their unfailing service.

All of these white knights of the education system depend greatly on the cynic who knows the price of everything and the value of nothing. The negative cultures depend on the cynic to provide them with the oxygen of negativity upon which they survive. Cynics can soak the lifeblood out of wherever they are found. They are the source of frustration and perspiration to the positive culture in any workplace.

You can provide more job enrichment and enlargement opportunities than there are in all the world, but to no avail. There comes a time when you have to leave the cynics and all their negative friends to their own world and move on without them. But not without a little victory. One tactic that worked with telling effect was what I called the *Procedures Uppercut question:* "What are due procedures in this instance?" Then again, I am sure there are many who would argue that I was wrong and that they were right on the premise that I was off on a crazy frolic with a group who subscribed to my line of thinking. A very good friend and work colleague described negative culture in an organisation: "They are the kind of people that if you show them a ring doughnut, they only see the hole!"

I remember as I waded into my first cycle of chemotherapy, and it was beginning to take its toll on me, that a member of staff asked to meet with me on the morning after a treatment. S/he proceeded to tell me directly what s/he would and would not do in his/her role in the school henceforth. In brief, s/he was giving me his/her "new" job description. I told him/her I understood what s/he was telling me and asked that s/he put his/her position in writing to the Board of Management for their earliest consideration in accordance with due procedures in this instance. After a short reflection, this person met with me again and advised me that s/he had reflected on our earlier meeting and suggested that it might be best if we could forget the stance that s/he had taken then. The *Procedures Uppercut* had worked with telling effect. S/he and others underestimated me. I might have been down in my health but there was more fight in the old dog yet.

Thankfully, I spent most of my life in positive cultures. I was fortunate enough to meet optimists who create coalitions of the willing in the workplace and to those people, nothing is impossible. They embrace opportunity and the greater the challenge, the more they enjoy it. I constantly surrounded myself with great and talented people who were intrinsically motivated, and in due course, their energy nurtured a positive culture in our work. You know that a positive culture dominates when you find certain people crossing over from the negative culture and celebrating achievements with the positive culture team, saying, "We did it." As they say, success has many parents, failure is always an orphan.

I learned more about and from the people I worked with during that time than I could possibly learn from lifetime of leadership seminars. Some of them were fabulous. There were times too when others tested my faith in people, when it was obvious that it was their goal to test my resolve. For example, I was assured of an ambush from certain quarters on the day after I had chemotherapy. It was like living in the midst of madness. Such assaults were led by those who at the best of times tended to be downright uninformed, crude and inarticulate with regard to policy, the democratic process, or the rules and procedures for primary schools. Their purpose was to incite discord and to undermine me at any given opportunity. Through my eyes, they saw my difficulty as their opportunity. I would like to think they learned that the reverse was true. I am told that I am a patient person and thankfully, I was assured by those who matter most to me that my leadership dexterity served me well.

Leading a team is always a challenge. I had to find the best way forward in calm and equally in troubled waters when the odds weighed unfavourably against me. Such assurances fuelled my engines and drove me on, mindful of Friedrich Nietzsche's dictum "That which doesn't kill us makes us stronger", and Ralph Waldo Emerson's "What lies behind us and what lies before us are tiny matters compared to what lies within us." As my idol Con Houlihan often wrote, "Now read on…"

It was suggested to me too that I might schedule my chemotherapy for outside of school hours because my absence from school for one day every three weeks was, apparently, disruptive to the running of the school. I explained that it would have been difficult to do this when the procedure began at nine in the morning and usually lasted until after five o'clock in the evening. Such attitudes made me even more determined not to play the cancer card. I would not underperform. I was determined to walk the walk regardless of my illness. Oh yes, I was the great pretender, pretending that I was doing fine. That was always my trump card when the going got tough - life had taught me to put the head down and drive on inspired by the mantra of Martin Farquhar Tupper, "Well timed silence has more eloquence than speech" and, "It is the mark of an educated mind to be able to entertain a thought without accepting it." – *Aristotle.* I hope I managed to achieve just that.

I was determined that nobody could point a finger at me and say that I was playing the cancer card to court sympathy and be excused for underperforming. There were many times when everything felt like an uphill struggle as the side-effects of the medication took their toll. I found myself trying to rationalise what was going on around me personally and professionally through a fog of confusion. Although my weary body struggled and my spirits wilted, I was determined not to give in. Stubborn to the end, I decided that every morning, I would get up, dress up, show up and keep my chin up – it was the best policy in the circumstances. Maybe that was arrogant of me, but I felt that if I was taking the wage packet, I was determined that nobody could or would point a finger at me and suggest that I wavered. Professional and personal pride was always important to me. There were days when anything that could go wrong did go wrong and I had to deal with it. That was the nature of my job. I had to deal with the "woodpeckers"; it was part of the job, although the purists would argue otherwise. It was my choice to be there and there was no way that I would hide from my responsibilities. I was determined to weather the storm. At times like these, I was driven on by the sense of Henry Ford's mantra, "When everything seems to be going against you, remember that the airplane takes off against the wind, not with it".

Externally, I presented as composed an image as possible and kept to myself the ravages of the chemical assault that was consuming me physically and emotionally. Inwardly, I was shattered and terrified. There were times when I felt so drained physically and emotionally that I felt that the world was imploding on me, dramatic though that may sound. I was not afraid of pain or whatever the treatment threw at me. I was more than terrified of dying. In the meantime, however, life had to go on and so it did. The sun rose every morning in the eastern sky and set every evening behind the western horizon. I went for chemotherapy every third week and those were my only absences from school during the cycle of treatment that lasted until June. It was a tough time for my family. Mary had to go to school and ensure that she was not distracted from her responsibilities to the students she taught. She had to have her exam classes primed and ready for exams in June. She would divulge later that she sought respite every morning in taking Buddy for his walk at 6.30 a.m. before she went to work. Nobody knew she was crying because she was walking in the dark and in the rain. Brian was in his final term in the University of Limerick and Ronan was preparing for his Leaving Certificate examination. Everybody had to get on with their lives. There was no place to hide. We resolved to face whatever the future held for us and deal with it as best we might. In times like these, I questioned the wisdom of the Irish proverb, "Is gaire cabhair Dé ná an doras" (God's help is closer than the door). There were times when I said to myself, "If this be true, the door must be very far away from us right now."

The snowdrops raised their little heads to signal that spring was on its way and they were followed by the daffodils, or the fair child of spring, as Oscar Wilde so aptly named them. The first flowers of spring were soon joined by crocuses, tulips, hyacinths, primroses, bluebells and others. Their scents combined to fragrance the breeze in which they tossed their heads and danced in the sunshine of springtime. These welcome signs did little to bring me solace from the internal war that was raging in my body as the chemotherapy battled 24/7 with the cancer. I saw the chemotherapy as the artillery that would attack and kill the parasite cancer that had invaded my body and was doing its utmost to eat the life out of me. I had to tell myself constantly that anything worthwhile is worth fighting for, and in this instance, it could be an unrelenting scrap to the end. Which would prevail, the cancer or me? For the battle field is no place for the faint hearted.

There were happy events that kept some semblance of normality in our lives. Ronan celebrated his seventeenth birthday on 30th January. His debs dance took place on 4th March at the Radisson Hotel. It was a welcome distraction as he and his friends were preoccupied with ensuring they had a partner for the great event. The boys and girls looked absolutely fabulous when they were decked out to perfection.

I had my third chemotherapy treatment on 23rd February. I passed the time on the IV reading *"More Than a Game; Selected Sporting Essays"* by one of my favourite journalists, Con Houlihan. He was one of Ireland's finest sportswriters. Over a lengthy career, he covered many of the greatest Irish and international sporting events, from classic Gaelic football and hurling finals, to the soccer and rugby world cups, the Olympics and numerous race meetings both in Ireland and abroad. He was a journalist with the Irish Press group and his columns in the Evening Press, until its demise in 1995, were compulsive reading. He also wrote fabulous columns on topics such as his exploits with Castleisland RFC, cutting turf, the delights of trout fishing and the poignancy of saying goodbye to the pigs before he went off to school in the knowledge that he would not see them again because they would be sold to the factory and gone into the food chain when he returned at the end of term. Con's columns in the Evening Press were a source of great discussion and entertainment to

Mary's late father, Dan Garvey and me for many years, and there were times when it was suggested that I won my father-in-law's favour through a mutual interest in the writings of his fellow county man, Con Houlihan.

Mary and her parents, Dan and Mary Garvey,
on the occasion of Mary's graduation in 1977.

I met with Professor Gupta when I was at the Cancer Centre that day for my third treatment, and he gave me the positive news that the molecular tests on my bone marrow were negative. It was cancer free. This was great news because as Professor Gupta explained to me, I now had the option of having my stem cells harvested for the future, should I ever need them. He seemed so favourably disposed to the prospect of harvesting that I was inclined in that direction also. His professional opinion was important to me and I found him to be a great source of support. The fact that my bone marrow was free from cancer was a great boost for my morale too, as the cumulative effects of the chemotherapy were taking exacting their price both mentally and physically. It was welcome news to my family also. Mary collected me from the hospital when the bone marrow aspiration procedure was completed that evening. When we got home, a colleague from work, Joanne O'Brien, delivered a cooked dinner for us. This was most thoughtful from a lady who is truly great in everything she does. Acts of kindness like this renewed our faith in the human spirit, together with visits from friends, relatives, colleagues from work, neighbours and messages of support. They all provided me with the energy and resilience to go on, even when the journey was uphill all the way and looked almost hopeless.

I had my fourth chemotherapy treatment on 16th March, as the swallows began to arrive from their winter habitat in North Africa to spend the summer months with us. They symbolised the beginning of spring and they filled the morning air with their twittering from lofty perches. This time, I occupied my hours in the Cancer Centre watching the Cheltenham Horse Racing Festival. There were some great followers of the sport of kings among us that day. Their enthusiasm was infectious as the horses were under starters' orders, as they approached the first up-and-over, together with moans and groans when there was a faller, not to mention the expletives whenever the faller was carrying a wager for some of the assembled patrons of the turf club.

I had a new and very frightening experience 21st March when I began to shake and shiver violently. I was terrified and thought the worst was about to happen to me, that I was about to die. Mary took me to the hospital. I was taken straight through at the outpatients section to where I was examined by a doctor and had my fears allayed. I had just experienced a severe bout of the rigors, which are a side-effect of the treatment I was receiving. When the doctor was satisfied that I was okay, I was allowed to go home. Although I had been advised to expect the rigors, they had until this stage taken the form of minor shakes and shivers, but nothing compared to the turbo version that had hit me on this occasion. The rigors made a habit of striking, and luckily, the more severe bouts chose to make their presence felt in the evening or at night when I was not at work. Every time they occurred subsequently, I had to go to the hospital immediately where I was checked out, and allowed home afterwards. I was able to go to school on the following morning as normal. I was taking life one step at a time and hoping for a favourable outcome.

Edel O'Doherty, a great friend of the family, celebrated her 21st birthday on 26th March. Needless to say, her party went on well beyond my bedtime so I took my leave while the young people and others who were young at heart marked the occasion with due celebration. I was taken aback a few nights after her party when she and her late mother, Geraldine, R.I.P., called to our house so that I would be present when Edel cut her birthday cake. It was a very touching gesture by both Edel and Geraldine. Little did any of us realise the fate that was in store for the O'Doherty family when Geraldine was diagnosed with cancer just three years later and passed away on 3rd March, 2009. Cancer struck them a cruel blow.

I had a CAT scan and my fifth session of chemotherapy on 6th April. The CAT scan would reveal if the chemotherapy was working. It was a long day in the hospital environment from leaving home at around 8 a.m. until I returned at 7 p.m. But it had to be done and there was nothing to be gained from complaining or feeling sorry for myself. I got the result of the CAT scan two days later and it showed that I was responding to the chemotherapy. I did not ask how great the response was; I was just happy that the news was encouraging. This hopeful news buoyed all of us and my mother felt that her prayers were being answered.

I had my sixth chemotherapy treatment on 27th April, as the voice of the wandering cuckoo arrived to fill the tree groves with song and news that summer was nigh. Trips to the Oncology Centre were now becoming a routine part of my life as a member of the cancer community. I kept telling myself that this was my sixth session and that after two more, I would be finished the course. With a ninety-five per cent success rate, there was latitude for cautious optimism. Mary collected me as usual in the evening when the procedure was completed and took me home. To add some light amusement to our evening, we noticed that I was unsteady on my feet in the same manner as if I'd had a few drinks too many. When I got home, the two boys joked how they suspected that I had spent the day in some hostelry or other.

Brian had a last fling with college life in April with RAG week. It was hard to believe that he was, at what might be described in the lexicon of the turf club, in the final straight in college and would shortly be taking his final exams. Rag week for the moment was a priority in his social calendar and the exams would be taken care of with due sufferance a month later in May.

The month of May was a busy one with Brian's final exams and Buddy's full hip-replacement operation. He (Buddy, not to be mistaken with Brian) had been diagnosed with hip dysplasia almost a year previously. We did our best to build up his muscles the previous year in August, September and October 2003 by taking him out to Killaloe and swimming in the lake with him. Despite our best efforts, he had to have surgery. He was admitted to Gilabbey Veterinary Clinic in Cork on Wednesday 25th May where they had an arrangement with a surgeon who travelled over from England especially to perform hip replacement operations. Buddy had surgery the following day, and we received regular updates on how well the operation had gone, when he woke from the anaesthetic, and how he was for the rest of the day. Mary collected him the next day and took him home where he was the primary focus of attention for some time. It was good to have a different patient under the spotlight for a change.

I had my seventh and second-last scheduled chemotherapy treatment on 18th May. This session brought an end to the era we had come to refer to as "Dancing in the Dark" because Bruce Springsteen's *Dancing in the Dark* was the soundtrack for Mary's arrival in Nenagh for work in the morning after dropping me to the Cancer Centre en route. Once she left me at the hospital for the day, she would play the *Best of Bruce Springsteen* collection to keep her company on the road and she always arrived in the school car park during the song *Dancing in the Dark.* She would be on summer holidays when the eighth session was due on 8th June.

The late Hunter S. Thompson's book, *Fear and Loathing in Las Vegas,* kept me company in the oncology ward for the duration of my treatment. By then, I was optimistic that the treatment was working and I looked forward to a favourable outcome from the CAT scan that was scheduled for me on completion of chemotherapy. The course of treatment and the school year were drawing to a close simultaneously. Around this time, I began negotiations with Dell Computers to secure some desktop computers for the school, as well as sourcing resources from benefactors. Pursuing projects like these lifted my spirits whenever I wilted in the journey – a journey that was taking its toll on both my family and me. We could put on appearances to the outside world, but we never shirked discussing the "undiscussables" between ourselves. We tried to be optimistic because we had to be; otherwise we would have gone crazy.

I convinced myself that the side effects of the treatment were minor discomforts on the road to the ultimate goal that was remission. I believed that the odds were in my favour. I had to believe that I would prevail. The alternative was unthinkable! The situation as I perceived it was that cancer invaded my body. Chemotherapy was my ally because it was infused into my body to fight our mutual enemy. I envisaged my body excreting the dead cancer cells. I believed in the process and it helped me to keep going.

The psychological and emotional battles were unrelenting. When I felt my body slowing and getting sluggish, I was determined not to capitulate and I fought with everything in me to make those hard yards when the going was tough. Mary, Brian and Ronan must have found me difficult to live with because I had to have been more cranky than usual as I felt my independence drain away from me. I found myself struggling in everything I did. I was moving more slowly, taking longer to get things done. My concentration was weaker and my powers of recall were not as sharp as they used to be. Although I was depending on my family to carry out tasks that until now I would get done at my ease, I was driven in the belief that this challenge was not impossible; I had just to try harder.

I had my final treatment of the first course of chemotherapy on 8th June as Ronan began his Leaving Certificate exam. I dropped him at school and went on to the hospital for treatment. It had to have been difficult enough for him facing his exam without the additional concerns he harboured about my health. However, he wanted me to leave him at the exam centre in keeping with the rituals of previous successful exams. I often wonder how he managed to do it at all. At the time, we just got on with life. The Leaving Cert was Ronan's passage out of post-primary school and, we hoped, on to college in September. Everyone has to cope with the challenges life presents to them. I consoled myself with the knowledge that Ronan would have his exams done and behind him in about a fortnight. It was poor consolation for him.

That day, I met a man at the Cancer Centre who was heartbroken because his prognosis was bad. He had pancreatic cancer and summarised his outlook by telling me that he would "not be around for the championship this year!" That shook me to the core and caused me to feel a lot less sorry for myself in advance of the CAT scan that was scheduled for 29th June, a scan that would ascertain whether the treatment had been successful. At least I had a 95%

chance of getting remission while this ill-fated man had zero prospects! Those are the harsh realities in the cancer community.

That unfortunate man was very much in my thoughts throughout the summer during the course of the inter-county hurling and football championships, and especially as the championships came to their conclusion in September.
I wondered whether he was still with his loved ones or if he too had departed like the swallows before the evening shadows of autumn grew longer and nature prepared to hibernate for winter.

Meanwhile, life did not stand still and Brian left Limerick on the 14th June bound for Australia - alone! It was a brave decision to travel on his own, but it allowed him the freedom to go where he chose and move on whenever he felt the inclination to do so. Brian called from Sydney on Saturday to touch base with us. We heard from him again five days later when he phoned from Brisbane to tell us that he had bought a car in the meantime for about 200 Australian dollars and driven it from Sydney to Brisbane. We were thrilled for him, young and full of life. He was riding his dreams like a thoroughbred.

From there, Brian went to Christchurch, New Zealand for the British and Irish Lions rugby test match against the New Zealand All Blacks. At this stage, I was spending some time familiarising myself with southern hemisphere geography trying to keep up with his travels! He arrived in Christchurch without a match ticket or pre-booked accommodation. When he was queuing for a taxi, he linked up with some other travellers who had a spare ticket and surplus accommodation because one of their travelling partners had not travelled as originally planned. Thus his accommodation and ticket requirements were sorted. The match was marred by the spear tackle on Brian O'Driscoll that caused him a very serious shoulder injury. The Lions were well beaten and the game was played in a downpour and Brian (Haugh) got soaked to the skin. His photo would later appear in a book published about the tour in which he was referred to as "the young lad from Limerick". Happy days!

Brian spent a few days sightseeing around Christchurch before returning to Australia. In mid-July, Mary received a letter from New Zealand and in it, there was a photo of Brian bungee jumping off the side of a mountain. Thank heavens he did not give us advance notice of his intentions on that occasion.

I got the CAT scan results on 7th July. To our dismay, the CAT scan revealed that I had only received part remission. That was a major disappointment because there was a 95% success rate with the course of treatment and here I was, one of the 5% for whom it had failed! This was bad news indeed, and no matter what way I looked at it, the future was bleak and very uncertain.

CHAPTER FIVE

Drifting With the Tide

"I wanted a perfect ending. Now I've learned, the hard way, that some poems don't rhyme, and some stories don't have a clear beginning, middle, and end. Life is about not knowing, having to change, taking the moment and making the best of it, without knowing what's going to happen next."

- Gilda Radner

At this decision point, it was settled that a course of wait and see was the preferred option for me – we would wait to see what the cancer might do next. Would it lie dormant? If it did, I would be okay as I was monitored regularly, and if it didn't lie dormant, the medical team would be at hand to deal with whatever emerged. It was a time of great uncertainty. I needed to be vigilant without becoming paranoid. It wasn't easy to achieve the balance and I am quite certain that I failed in this regard, although I tried my best at the time. It was hard to differentiate between the minor aches that might occur in the body from time to time, and symptoms of what might be a return of the dreaded cancer.

Embarking on the wait-and-see part of the journey was not ideal. I had hoped to avoid it because to my mind, it was a case of waiting to see what the cancer would do next. It's analogous to dealing with a volcano in that one has to wait and see if it remains dormant and inactive, if it instead becomes active, and if so, how active might it become? What were the chances of a favourable outcome if and when it became active again and I had more chemotherapy? All the answers were in those three words - wait and see.

We found it difficult to accept the results of the scan. Brian was in Australia and it was not easy to break the unpleasant news to him. It was equally difficult to bring the dismal tidings to Ronan. He had just finished his Leaving Certificate and instead of a carefree summer, he was surrounded with the uncertainty that cancer had introduced to all our lives. Brian had phoned us from Australia soon after we came out from the hospital to enquire about the scan results. It was a most difficult situation; we had to tell him the truth and knowing he was alone so far away from home without support made a heart-breaking situation even worse. Obviously, he was very upset and disappointed. We would learn from him later that it was a particularly bad evening in Noosa, located about 130 kilometres north of Brisbane in the Sunshine Coast region of South East Queensland, Australia. While he tried to cope with the outcome of my scan, his fellow travellers from England were trying to make contact with friends and family back home in the aftermath of the terrorist attack in London.

Mary and I were shattered. We were very upset for Brian and equally, Ronan. The future, if there was going to be a future, looked very grim no matter what kind of spin one tried to put on it. It was another one of those days when hope and optimism deserted us. My life seemed to be going down a series of dead-end streets. The sense of helplessness and hopelessness seemed to get worse and worse. The situation was out of control and there was nothing I could do about it. Things had never been as unfavourably disposed for me in life as they seemed right now, and the odds were stacked against me; part remission meant that the other side of the scales was weighing over with failure. Things were pretty bad whatever way I looked at it and I knew that sometime in the future, the cancer would strike again. I think all of us knew, and there was no point in trying to delude ourselves. While we processed the result of the scan, we had to get on with whatever other trials and tribulations the day might bring us. In advance of any further challenges, we decided to have lunch and compose ourselves before I went to join members of the school staff who were attending a summer in-service training course. We ordered lunch, but we did not eat it; not because of any dissatisfaction. We were devastated again.

While we sat looking into our lunches, my phone flashed to let me know that I had missed two calls from an Ennis number. I returned the calls, only to realise that they were from the Clare Education Centre, where I had done an interview earlier in the week for a job with Leadership Development for Schools. I had applied for the job more out of curiosity to see how I might perform at interview than out of ambition. Well, it now appeared that I had impressed the interview panel because they offered me the position of Assistant National Co-ordinator. Although the title of the job on offer was impressive, my initial reaction was to decline it. However, after due consultation and consideration, I decided to accept the offer. My decision was influenced in no small way by the scan results. Suddenly, I wanted to take myself out of the school because I did not want to be among the children and school community when (as now seemed inevitable) the cancer would return. Although there were no major or obvious physical changes in me throughout the first cycle of chemotherapy, I was fairly certain that future treatments would not be kind in that regard. Most of all, I did not want the school children watching me decline physically under the effects of the next round of chemotherapy, which would probably be more severe. Equally, I did not want my illness to become a spectator sport within the school community and its wider audience.

When I joined the staff that day, they were disappointed to hear the scan results and it was simply a very awkward situation for all of us. Really, what does one say in the circumstances? It's not like you can say what you're thinking! One staff member suggested to me that I was probably overreacting while another opined that I would be okay after a few brandies. If only it were that simple. Life needed to go on whatever the future held for me and my family and so we all wished each other a pleasant summer holiday and went our separate ways.

I went to Ennis to meet the people from Leadership Development for Schools (LDS) who were offering me a job. I was upfront with them on the health issue as I had been at interview. They still offered me the job. I thought these were either supreme optimists or badly stuck in their search for staff, taking me on in such uncertain health circumstances. To cut a long story short, I took the job and decided to make the best of whatever was to come.

I had a troubled mind and a heavy heart throughout the summer. Although I did my best not to wear my concerns on my sleeve, cancer was never far from my thoughts. Deep within me, I had a foreboding that I would have another encounter with cancer. After all, I was on a wait-and-see phase in the process, which I interpreted as waiting to see what the cancer would do next. I was not going to delude myself thinking and hoping that it would go away, or evaporate like the morning dew. It was going to strike again; the burning questions were when, where and how? Cancer was out there in the long grass replenishing its reserves, waiting for its opportunity to strike when it could inflict maximum damage. I knew that when it struck again, it might be more challenging than it had been previously. The next round of chemotherapy would most likely cause significant changes in my physical appearance. To that end, I kept myself busy and did my best to be inspired by my late father's philosophy:

"In life's daily tasks, let this be your guide: It is better to keep trying, than sitting and sighing, and awaiting the tide!"

Summer rolled on. Ronan completed his Leaving Cert and Mary got the school timetable done. Ronan got a summer job with Mick Kemmy at his shop, Stonecraft, in the Tait Centre in the city. He was enjoying his summer work and the sense of relief that comes from finishing exams. All of a sudden, he began to feel unwell and complained of stomach pains. Mary took him to the doctor on Saturday 2nd July. He was sent to hospital for observation where he was put on a drip and fasted overnight. To his dismay he was kept under observation over the weekend and then eventually discharged on the Monday with a clean bill of health in good time to prepare himself for the Oxegen festival. He survived it and it survived him!

Ronan left home to join Brian in Australia on Sunday 24th July for their much-planned reunion and subsequent adventures. On our way to Dublin Airport, Ronan commented that "things were back to normal" with me doing the driving. That remark rocked me! Thankfully, I was showing some external signs of returning to normal, in his eyes at least. It meant a lot to Ronan and that made me feel good. I hoped that the positivity he was experiencing would be a good sign to Brian when they met up down under. People questioned our judgment as parents in sending a seventeen-year-old to the other end of the world on his own. Maybe we were irresponsible. But somehow, he and Brian had hatched the plan months earlier and they deserved the opportunity to live the dream. Mary and I have always subscribed to the philosophy that life is not a dress rehearsal; you get one chance at it and then it is over. We don't do regrets. My late father, Jackie's mantra, "*It is better to be sorry for doing it than sorry for not doing it*" has always fuelled this attitude in me.

On Monday 25th July, my mother came to spend some time with us. We passed the following evening on the computer tracking the last leg of Ronan's journey from Singapore to Brisbane. Out of the blue, the phone rang. It was Brian asking us to make contact with Ronan to tell him that he (Brian) could not go into the airport to meet him because he had to keep the engine of the car running outside due to mechanical problems. Mary and I hid out in the kitchen to spare my mother the anxiety as she watched television in the family room, oblivious to the communication challenges that were emerging for her grandchildren in the Southern Hemisphere. The next 90 minutes were spent in the kitchen trying to get messages to Ronan. In the end, I felt like Radar in M.A.S.H. relaying messages to and from one to the other. Those who disapproved of Ronan's solo trip to join Brian would have had a field day if only they had seen us.

At 11.10 p.m., I finally made telephone contact with Ronan after much effort. He had reached the arrivals area of Brisbane Airport and was relieved to hear from me because he was having difficulty making contact with Brian. Meanwhile, Mary was on her phone to Brian who was doing circuits of the car park to keep his car engine running. Brian issued instructions to Mary that she relayed to me. Then in turn, I relayed the message to Ronan that he should leave the airport through exit number four and that Brian would pick him up the next time he was passing that point on his circuit. Then, suddenly I heard the honking of a car horn and Ronan shouting, "Oh, I see him, I see him! Goodbye!" Such relief! Alexander Graham Bell's initial innovation in telecommunications in 1876 that laid the first foundations for the twenty-first century medium enabled Brian and Ronan to be united, while Henry Ford's invention proved somewhat temperamental on the night!

We returned to the family room to join my mother after solving our sons' connectivity problems, only to have her extol the virtues of the two boys. She waxed eloquent on their independence and levelheadedness for the best part of an hour. Just as well that she was unaware of the situation that played out between them in Brisbane Airport just moments earlier,,,

I spent July in part remission, waiting to find out if the Board of Management of the school would release me on secondment to take up the job on offer from LDS. There were those who both supported me and hindered me in doing what I thought was best for me then. It was a learning experience. Some suggested that I was turning my back on the school and letting down its staff and pupils if I took up the offer. But the decision was in the hands of the Board of Management. As far as I was concerned, Mahatma Gandhi had it right: "Nobody can hurt me without my permission."

George Kimball, American author and sports columnist, and his wife Marge Marash came to visit us for a few days at the end of July. Marge assured us that while I did not get a full remission from cancer, it was a huge bonus to know that the cancer had not reached my bone marrow. We enjoyed their company and they proved a welcome distraction from medical matters. The Limerick Leader did a feature interview with George and published it in the weekend edition of the paper. George had some tests in autumn when he returned to New York and was himself diagnosed with cancer. It was a shattering blow for him and his family. George did not see himself as a victim. On the contrary, he kept himself busy and through 2008, 2009 and 2010, he managed to maintain a presence, beat the odds, and pop up at big fights and golf tournaments on both sides of the Atlantic. From the time he was diagnosed until he died on the 6th July 2011, he had five books published as an author and editor. One of them, *American at Large,* in 2008, was a collection of columns from The Irish Times. He launched it in Dublin in July 2008 and co-dedicated it to his foursome from hell; Finbar Fury, Kevin Haugh, Pat Ruddy and Niall Toibín, to which he added "May they continue to lead me astray..."

We learned with great sadness that George passed away on the 6th July, 2011 in New York. Although we knew he was very, very ill and his time was drawing to a close, it is hard to imagine life without him. He was good-hearted, kind, generous and just plain fun to be around. Anyone who read his work could appreciate his enormous talent. You had to know him to appreciate that he was the full package, always busy living. He never wasted a minute of his time and he lived life to the full, engaging everyone around him in whatever he did. Despite his hectic schedule, he never seemed to be in a great hurry and gave generously of his time to all of us. I was mesmerised by George's attention to detail in everything he did, whether in his writings or in general conversation. He had no peers. We were lucky to have shared life's journey with him, and his departure has left a void that all of us will feel, but none more so than his wife Marge, daughter Darcy and son Teddy.

Bob Ryan wrote in the Boston Globe 9th July, 2011, "George Kimball extracted every last ounce of life out of Life. He was the kind of guy around whom myths abounded." George my good friend, thanks for the memories and the good times we had together. Rest in peace.

Cancer is like a parasite that lurks in dark alleys waiting to jump you when you least expect it. It is not selective about where and whom it strikes. It seeks and destroys. It is merciless and displays absolute contempt for its prey. It invades the body and wreaks physical and mental havoc on it day and night. It never sleeps. Battling cancer is difficult. I have felt robbed of my independence and my life is more uncertain. I've learned to live from one medical appointment to the next. There were days before each appointment when I felt like I was waiting for the jury to come to a decision on whether to commute my sentence!

In July, 2005, I got back into doing a little jogging twice or three times a week. Really, it was more of a shuffle than jogging, but it was an effort to give my life some semblance of what I wanted it to be. I started with one mile and built it up to two miles. There was never a danger of me breaking land speed records in my running rehabilitation programme. My lungs ached as I gasped for air and plunged into oxygen debt. In local rugby parlance, this condition is referred to as "sucking seagulls". Nevertheless, it was a major psychological victory to get into my running gear again, even though I now weighed fourteen stone and ten pounds (ninety-four kilos), more than a full stone heavier than what I'd weighed twelve months earlier. My weight gain didn't bother me. I was never cover-page material so there was no loss of royalties in that quarter! I was alive and when I had a check-up in the hospital on 4th August, the medical team was happy with my condition. Things looked so good that my next appointment was scheduled for the end of October, which was ten weeks away. An air of optimism folded round us once again!

News from Australia was encouraging too; Brian and Ronan were driving up along the east coast of Australia from Sydney to Cairns, and they were having the time of their lives. Their exploits took them snorkelling on the Great Barrier Reef as well as swimming with sharks somewhere along the coast. They assured us that the sharks survived and suffered no ill effects of their encounter with the boys. Meanwhile, Brian got his final exams results from the University of Limerick and was scheduled to graduate in September. Ronan got his Leaving Cert. results and secured a place in Law and Accounting at the University of Limerick. Life felt good again!

On 22nd August, I noticed that I had less energy than normal and the alarm bells rang when I struggled to swim even one length of a swimming pool. My fears were soon compounded when I noticed a swelling in the left side of my neck a few days later and I began to suffer severe lower abdominal pain. The pains got progressively worse and I arranged an appointment with Professor

Gupta for Thursday, 1st September. In the meantime, I had a briefing regarding a stem cell harvesting procedure in St. James's Hospital in Dublin on 30th August. It was explained to me that success in this endeavour was not a foregone conclusion as there were several variables that could cause failure. They took blood samples for analysis in advance to ascertain if stem cell harvesting was feasible in my case. It was a long journey home by train as I pondered whether I had a future or not. The dark clouds of fear gathered.

CHAPTER SIX

Perfect Storms, No Compass

"What counts is not necessarily the size of the dog in the fight, what counts is the size of the fight in the dog."

-   Mark Twain

August and September signal the beginning of Mary's and my work year. Every year is different and this one was particularly so. The cancer in my body had changed from a slow growing to a fast growing form. Coming to terms with the demands of work while coping with cancer was blowing my mind. Nevertheless, I had to present a cool exterior, deliver on the work front, keep the home fires burning and maintain as much calm as possible.

Brian started his training contract in Chartered Accounting with Norman O'Leary & Company in Limerick City. Ronan progressed from post-primary school to third level at the University of Limerick. At least their academic lives were staying on course. Mary went to work every day and I did likewise. We were very ordinary people on the exterior and there are many like us juggling daily routines of work and coping with what life throws at them from the blindside. Life went on just as cooler breezes told of summer's fading and we had to keep pace with it. It was a case of "Stop pedalling and you fall off the bike!"

I had an appointment with Professor Gupta on 1st September and he decided that we would adopt a wait-and-see approach for the time being. I was comfortable with his decision because he went to great lengths to explain the reasons for the course of action he was adopting, and I had absolute confidence in his professional judgment. Meanwhile, I kept trying to convince myself that the lump in my neck was due to the throat infection that I had. However hard we tried to delude ourselves, there was no persuading my mother.

I immersed myself in my new job. I had my first team meeting with LDS during the week and it looked like a busy year ahead. We had to plan and design materials for the induction of newly appointed principals, as well as programmes to meet the continued professional development requirements of experienced school leaders throughout the country.

On Wednesday, 7th September, my worst fears were realised when I phoned St. James's Hospital to enquire about my blood test results. They informed me that the tests showed that the LDH was up, which indicated that there was some level of cancer in my system and it would compromise the stem cell harvesting process. This was bad news for me because at that stage I was relapsing, and the lifeline of having my own stem cells harvested to be transplanted back into me if the occasion arose was drifting out of my reach. The signs were not favourable. Just as the autumn shadows of evening grew longer, my prospects contracted menacingly.

I was left with an empty pain in the pit of my stomach. I felt as if my last train had left the station and that I had joined the wrong queue. The long cold sleep beckoned. The angels of death were closing in on me like hungry coyotes, mocking me with shrieks of their laughter. I was overwhelmed by my prospects and tormented with thoughts of who might look out for my family when I ceased to be. I might not be much good, I thought to myself, but surely I was better than nothing? Any way I looked at it, I was not ready *to go!* This was real life theatre and I was bang in the middle of it and to make matters worse, this play was all about my life ebbing away and I was helpless to stem the flow of the tide. Once again, I felt like somebody looking in on all of this playing itself out as I approached a state of physical and emotional paralysis.

Up until now, the stem cell therapy procedure had offered me the preferred option of using my own stem cells, which would reduce the risk of rejection associated with using second party stem cells, such as the ones procured from a stem cell bank or family member. My sister, Josephine (O'Neill), offered to be a potential donor should the occasion arise. The success rate in using donor stem cells was not as high as when the patient's own cells were harvested and transplanted. There was also some considerable risk that Josephine and I might not be compatible, and consequently, she would not be a suitable donor. It was a time of great stress and uncertainty. It was not a time to show the panic I was feeling internally.

It appeared to me that my prospects were diminishing rapidly and that the situation was out of control. I waited impatiently and with a sense of dread for St. James's Hospital to ring me back regarding the options available to me in light of my blood test results.

They did not phone me until late in the evening, by which time I had made contact with the cancer liaison nurse in the Mid-Western Oncology Unit, who told me that I had been given misinformation about the harvesting option. Relief! For once in my life I was relieved to hear that I had been given inaccurate information from whoever phoned me from St. James's Hospital earlier in the day. The cancer liaison nurse in the Mid-Western Oncology Unit in Limerick told me that Professor Gupta wanted to meet with me first thing next morning to reassure me that my situation had not been compromised and that the harvesting would go ahead as planned. This information brought renewed hope. Thankfully, I had worked through this scenario on my mobile without causing further stress to my family.

I met Professor Gupta and the cancer liaison nurse as scheduled the following morning before 9 a.m., and they allayed my fears by showing me all the paperwork in which my harvesting procedure was agreed with St. James's Hospital. Professor Gupta advised that I would have a CAT scan and a biopsy immediately, and that he would schedule my harvesting to take place as soon as possible. I travelled to Tullamore for a work-related meeting the next day, and in the evening, I received a phone call from the cancer liaison nurse to inform me that I had an appointment on Monday, 12th September to prepare for the biopsy. I would have a CAT scan on Friday 16th. It was all systems go with the medical team. It was "beginning to look a lot like Christmas" in more ways than one. In some ways, it was not unlike the previous year when I was diagnosed shortly before Christmas. The medical team had wasted no time in ensuring that I got the best medical care without a moment's delay, and somehow, I found reason to believe that I would survive and together we would prevail in our mission against the mutual enemy, cancer. It was times like this that taught me to cling to anything that might bring the desired outcome.

Squeezed in among appointments, Brian graduated from the University of Limerick on Tuesday, 13th September, 2005. While it was a great family event, I realised that night how, despite all the outward signs of celebration, the day had served to bring to the surface the thoughts of dread that Ronan was harbouring. He called me aside for a private chat.

He asked me to promise him that I would fight the cancer and be around in 2009 for his graduation. It was a chilling moment! Choked with emotion he handed me the following poem by Dylan Thomas:

Do Not Go Gentle into That Good Night

Do not go gentle into that good night,
Old age should burn and rave at close of day;
Rage, rage against the dying of the light.

Though wise men at their end know dark is right,
Because their words had forked no lightning they
Do not go gentle into that good night.

Good men, the last wave by, crying how bright
Their frail deeds might have danced in a green bay,
Rage, rage against the dying of the light.

Wild men who caught and sang the sun in flight,
And learn, too late, they grieved it on its way,
Do not go gentle into that good night.

Grave men, near death, who see with blinding sight
Blind eyes could blaze like meteors and be gay,
Rage, rage against the dying of the light.

And you, my father, there on that sad height,
Curse, bless, me now with your fierce tears, I pray.
Do not go gentle into that good night.
Rage, rage against the dying of the light.

Burning with a desire to fulfil his one request, I promised him that I would win the battle with cancer to be with him on his graduation day. Brave talk, you might say, or even that it was downright irresponsible of me. Maybe so, as I could have been accused of making an outlandish promise in the circumstances and of giving my son false hope. Fair enough. However, which of us can make a promise that we can be certain of keeping? Life is riddled with uncertainty and I was faced with giving Ronan hope or despair. I chose the only thing I had to give him then, and that was hope. The promise was given more in hope than in confidence because things were going from bad to worse. At times like these in the journey, I felt that whoever coined Murphy's Law was an optimist.

I had my medical appointment on Monday and the biopsy was scheduled for Thursday of the following week. I was kept in hospital on Thursday night after the biopsy procedure and had a CAT scan on the next day, Friday. Professor Gupta called to see me on Friday morning and told me that he would have the results of my scan and biopsy when he met me the following week when I had returned from Dublin after the stem cell harvesting. I passed my time in hospital attending to enquiries from work and programme design.

I was started on a course of injections to stimulate the bone marrow in advance of the stem cell harvest. The injections were for three or four days with a mobilisation factor. These shots caused the stem cells from the marrow to go into the blood stream in preparation for the stem cell harvesting. I practiced giving myself the injections under the supervision of the medical team in advance of being discharged from hospital on Saturday at 5 p.m. It was good to get home albeit for only twenty-four hours before I set off for Dublin with our neighbour and good friend, Gerry Berkery. Gerry was on his way to a business appointment while I was going for a stem cell harvesting procedure. I managed to stay in touch with work all the while.

I had an early morning appointment for a blood test in St. James's Hospital on the next day, Monday 19th, that would determine if the stem cell count test was adequate to allow harvesting. Afterwards, I returned to the hotel where I kept my mind occupied by immersing myself in my work. This was one particular situation in which I was happy to be busy. I got a telephone call at 2.05 p.m. from the hospital with the disappointing news that the stem cell count was not high enough to carry out a harvesting procedure. This was a setback. Two failures and I would be struck out of the harvesting schedule. I was rescheduled for an early-morning test again the next day. Mary, Brian and Ronan were disappointed to hear that harvesting did not take place. However, we were becoming accustomed to setbacks and the need to bounce back in the face of adversity. I re-immersed myself in work until well into the evening.

My friend Michael Downes joined me on Monday and helped me to pass the time. Michael is originally from West Clare and now lives in Dublin. We drank lots of tea and chatted for a few hours. I appreciated the company as it helped to take my mind off medical matters and the uncertainty that every day brought. We managed to keep our conversation on a positive vein and remained upbeat about my medical condition. It wasn't that I was afraid of discussing it; it was more that I was tired of thinking and talking about cancer and I welcomed an opportunity to talk about something else. I also believed that for some people it was analogous to the catchphrase "Don't mention the war," because they wanted to talk about anything other than sickness, and that was a welcome respite for me too.

Before I turned in for the night, I worked really hard on filling my mind with a positive and aggressive attitude towards fighting the cancer that had invaded my body, and I know this sounds like brave talk from a person who was terrified of dying. Whether there was a life hereafter, I wasn't inclined to go and find out. Anybody who had already gone stayed there and I was not ready for a permanent move just yet.

Equally, the influence of the older generation inspired me, and my determination to survive was fuelled by the wisdom of the late Joe Quinlan Senior, a neighbour of ours in West Clare in the early 1960s. I remember my late father, Jackie, telling how Joe was very ill a few years before he passed away. Subsequently, in the course of a conversation, my father mentioned to him that he (Joe) had made a great recovery. Joe replied, in his inimitable manner, "Sure Jackie, not even the little mouse wants to die - doesn't he put up a great fight to get away from the cat to stay alive?" Joe passed away a few years later when I was about seven years old. In my own way, I was like the mouse. I didn't want to die and I had to do what was required of me in the circumstances to stay alive. Words of wisdom from yesteryear learned from the University of Life and handed down from generation to generation served me well almost half a century later. They were truly great people and we should never forget them.

To be strictly honest, I was neither amused nor enamoured by the prospect of dying and ceasing to be for evermore! The only option for me was the Munster rugby team mantra: "Stand Up and Fight" as valiantly as I could and hope that the dreaded final bell would not toll prematurely. The thoughts of lying there dead, Mary, Brian and Ronan together with my mother in a funeral home saying goodbye to me for the last time, and I lying there about to be buried or cremated the following day, left me cold. That would be the end of me. No more tomorrows, just a tombstone, an urn or ashes scattered somewhere in the wind! I had to press on with the business of staying alive before the gremlins caught up with me. I pumped my mind with images as I visualised my body producing the stem cells to meet the requirements of the stem cell test count in the morning that would allow for the procedure to go ahead. I was reminded of a quotation from Ernest Hemmingway, "Enthusiasm is not enough". I realised that enthusiasm would not be enough to see me over the line on this occasion. It was a case of fight or die and I urged my body to answer the call for one last herculean effort. There was no margin for error. This was a life or death situation. I commanded my body to produce the stem cells!

I attended for the blood test next morning as planned. It was a long wait until I returned to the hospital at 12.30 p.m. to be informed that the stem cell count was within the range for harvesting. I was briefed again on the procedures. I had two large IV lines inserted into the veins of both arms. The blood was taken out of my left arm and it went through a machine that extracted the stem cells before the blood was returned to my body through a line inserted in my right arm.

I had to lie perfectly still for three hours while the procedure was taking place because any movement would cause the process to collapse. Failure was not an option. There was no margin for error in this part of the process. I could not afford to move a limb. As I understood it, I was in serious trouble and my chances of survival would implode if this procedure failed. It was unnerving to think that my life had turned into a series of procedures aimed at evading death. This was my last chance at the stem cell harvest so I had to give it everything. I put myself in the zone through deep concentration. Thankfully, I stayed in the zone and managed to stay absolutely still for the duration of the procedure.

Once I got over the first inclinations to scratch my nose or rub my forehead, I managed to focus on the mission in hand. I summoned the powers of my mind to transport myself to a place of great beauty, to the world that nurtured the imagination of my childhood. Once again, I was a child in *Tír na nÓg* (an imaginary land of eternal youth).
It was a magical world where I met with and was comforted by all the creatures of the environment. I was reminiscent of Dr. Doolittle as I walked and talked to the birds and the animals. Each of them had a story to tell and I had all day to listen.

When the procedure was completed, the medical team had to recall me from the wonder-world into which I had escaped, where time passed quickly and I experienced no discomfort. At the end of the three hours I was elated. I was halfway there. The good news gave a much needed lift to my family at home, to my mother, and to those who were supporting us on this unenviable journey.

I had to repeat the procedure again the next day because I needed two successful harvests. I spent the evening and night playing all sorts of mind games in my efforts to get my body to generate stem cells for another successful outcome on the next day. I talked to myself and called on my body to work hard with me. I visualised a light burning from the sky in which my Heavenly Mother sent energy into my veins, stimulating growth in the stem cells. I talked to my body in the second person telling it that it was capable of getting over the line as it had done in previous challenges. I drew on the many experiences I'd had during my journey through life in which I'd felt overwhelmed and somehow managed to keep my head down and get over them. This challenge was different because cancer eats at you until it eventually breaks down your body, and dismantles you until you finally succumb. It is vicious and merciless. Nevertheless, I kept telling myself that the only option was to fight my way out of this corner. I drew on my marathon experiences when I would talk to myself whenever I was going through a difficult patch in a race. I relied on the lessons I learned over the years when my whole world looked like it was falling apart. I talked myself through those challenges. It was my way of dealing with life, my insecurities, rejection, failure and everything that caused me to struggle when I was a child, teenager, young man, middle-aged man and now, a sick man.

D-day dawned for me. Today, Ronan would start his third-level education in the University of Limerick and I needed to have another successful harvest with a targeted amount of between 2 million and 2.5 million stem cells per kilogram body weight for effective transplantation. I was in the hospital at 8.30 a.m. and hooked up to the machine for harvesting. I really went for it. I put myself into deep meditation again and visualised myself en route back to *Tír na nÓg*, where I had been the previous day. I concentrated on transporting my awareness above the gravity of the procedure and brought my mind and body to a relaxed state. I achieved this by telling myself that I was going to have a very enjoyable experience in a land where all creatures great and small communicated and lived in total harmony. The fish swam, dolphins played, birds sang and the animals frolicked in the sunshine while Buddy kept court with all quarters. He was in ecstasy when we swam with the dolphins until suddenly I felt a sudden sensation. Although it broke a moment of magic, it was a welcome intrusion from the medical staff to tell me that the procedure was finished. They were interested in the strategy I employed because they noticed that it totally relaxed my body and allowed for a smooth and non-eventful procedure on both occasions. I explained that I had engaged in a visualisation or meditation exercise, but did not elaborate lest they conclude that I was absolutely crazy, a danger to myself and humankind, and in need of immediate incarceration in the best interests of my own safety!

I tried to relax and spent the time reading until 2.15 p.m. when they told me that the harvest had been successful. I had recorded 2.21 million stem cells per kilogram body weight for effective transplantation. Mission accomplished! I was on the next train home from Dublin, happy and relieved. On my journey home, the man I met on June 8th in the Cancer Centre came to mind and I wondered if he got to watch the championship and how life might been for him and his family over the summer months. Brian met me at the train station and it was great to be home again. The next day was Brian's birthday so we had double cause for celebration. Around this time, I noticed that our dog Buddy, who is a golden retriever, was becoming ever more aware of the fluctuations of my energy levels. There were times when he certainly went to great lengths to entertain me or simply lie by my feet whenever my energy levels were low.

"It's not whether you get knocked down; it's whether you get up."

- Vince Lombardi

We got on with life and work. I also had to try and keep my mother from worrying about me. Work took me all over the country, which was a blessing in disguise because it kept me occupied professionally. It was not a time for self-pity or tardiness. There was a job to be done and I told myself that I had to get it done. An experience at a venue in Waterford made episodes of *Fawlty Towers* seem very tame by comparison. The roof leaked and buckets were placed under each drop down. The conference organiser in the hotel suggested that the participants be asked to seat themselves between the leaks from the roof. The situation was crazy at best. I took immediate action to have our accommodation changed. I had to increase my skills of negotiation from conciliatory to more assertive to secure an immediate upgrade. I convinced myself that it was all part of the job.

I had an evening appointment with Professor Gupta on Tuesday, 26th September, and our worst fears were realised. The cancer had changed from a slow-growing to an aggressive form called Diffuse Large B Cell, which would mean more chemotherapy without undue delay. We had to compose ourselves as best we could and ask that treatment commence as soon as possible. Professor Gupta wasted no time and arranged for me to have my first treatment the next morning. Nothing was ever a problem to him in the best interest of my healthcare. He treated me as if I was the only patient in the world, and he consistently had my medical needs attended to immediately without fuss or delay.

We were tossed and thrown again as a family in our rollercoaster ride with cancer. There was nothing we could do but brace ourselves for the uncertain challenges that lay ahead. The trees in their autumn beauty and the harvest moon were among the few modicums of solace from the mood of doom that consumed me. The swallows were well on their way to the land where *Eoghainín na nÉan* said it is always summer. I hoped that I would have emerged from the repair shop in good enough shape to welcome them back in the springtime.

CHAPTER SEVEN

Coasting in Fog

"Hope never abandons you; you abandon it."

- George Weinberg

The same routines as before applied for the September to December cycle of chemotherapy, although I felt that this time we were dancing in a different dark - on a more downward curve. The first treatment of the autumn schedule was on 28th September. Returning to the Cancer Centre was difficult. The disappointment of the scan in June and the return of a more aggressive form of cancer made my survival more precarious. The medical team was outstanding. They were sensitive to my vulnerabilities and their support was second to none, especially at times like this when it seemed to me that I was fast heading for rock bottom. The procedure began with blood tests followed by infusion of the chemotherapy.

Mary collected me at 5 p.m. after her day's work at school. I was tired and unsteady on my feet that evening, which alerted me to the fact that this course was stronger than the one I'd had earlier in the year from January to June. I got up the next morning and went to work even though I felt terrible. I had to inject myself that evening with a white blood stimulant. It was not very long before I realised that the previous course of chemotherapy was a picnic compared to this one.

My taste buds were affected again by the chemotherapy and everything tasted of lead and aluminium. My energy levels dropped progressively. There were extremes from constipation to diarrhoea; bouts of nausea, abdominal pain, blinding headaches, blurred vision, and difficulty concentrating as the cumulative effects of the chemotherapy proved unrelenting. Once more, I was living with the feeling of a permanent hangover. The night sweats were worse than ever and sometimes it felt like I was sleeping in a swamp. The foul body odour got worse, and I reached a stage where the painkillers brought no relief whatsoever. It was a case of having to fight on and make the best of the situation. I worked late into the evenings and at night, as well as on Saturdays and Sundays to make sure that I kept ahead of my work schedule. It was my way of doing the best I could.

I had my second treatment of the autumn cycle of chemotherapy during the second week in October, and Professor Gupta seemed reasonably pleased with my progress. He told me that I would continue with the present course until early December. Then I would have a series of tests to ensure that I was in a fit condition in preparation for high-dose chemotherapy that would commence on 4th January in the Regional Hospital, Dooradoyle. After that, I would have a stem cell transplant on January 10th and 11th in St. James's Hospital, Dublin. He also informed me that I would be in hospital for between three and a half and four weeks for the procedure. Once again, I realised that I was in the best possible medical care available anywhere in the world. Professor Gupta and his team were in constant watch of my situation and kept me informed of their plan of action.

Soon after my second treatment of chemotherapy, my hair began to fall out in clumps, so I decided it would be best to have my head shaved. Unfortunately, for Brian, I asked him to do it for me and he obliged with great bravery. In retrospect, I realise that I should not have asked him to do it and should have either done it myself or gone to the barber. Hindsight is everything. It was not the loss of what hair I had that was traumatic, but the circumstances in which I had to lose it. My judgement calls were seriously flawed in matters like this, especially as time went on. I also found myself struggling with everything that required physical effort or long-term concentration. There were times even in conversation when I felt as if I were drifting away, or into a haze from which I found it extremely difficult to return. I planned my driving very carefully in order to ensure that I was alert and never put others or myself in danger.

It was tough going but I wasn't inclined to yield as I braced myself for whatever emerged over the next few phases of the journey. On 17th October, I had to start a course of EPO to promote red cell growth. This procedure meant that I had to inject myself as directed by a nurse who called to my home and showed me how it was done. It was a straightforward procedure and I managed it without any problem. That same evening, I decided to phone a man whom I befriended when both of us were in hospital in September to catch up with him and enquire how life was with him. To my great shock, the person who answered the phone was his son. He told me that his father had passed away suddenly on the previous Thursday and was laid to rest at the weekend. You think you are having a bad day until you hear how life is treating other people.

While the EPO injections promoted the growth of red blood cells, I also had to inject myself with a white blood cell stimulant. The white blood cell stimulant caused terrible bone pain about ten days after the injection. The pains got worse, and even stronger doses of morphine failed to bring relief as time went on. It was all part of the treatment and there was no point in complaining or whinging. I was very much aware that I needed to remain focused on fighting the cancer. There were times when it was more difficult than others; nevertheless I was determined not to wilt under the pressure. I remembered the words of our good neighbour from West Clare, Joe Quinlan (Junior) when he said, "Kevin, you must fight it; you owe it to yourself and your family." He was right!

There were many side effects. I got a particularly bad bout of the rigors on the night of 19th October when I stayed in the Temple Gate Hotel in Ennis. I had a meal in the restaurant with some of the LDS team before turning in for the night. During the meal I felt unwell and took my leave discreetly when an opportunity presented itself. At about 2 a.m., I woke with terrible pains in my body. I got up and walked around the room and rolled about on the floor but the pain only got progressively worse. Before long, I was in agony. The pain was probably the worst I had ever experienced in my life. I was certain that it was the beginning of the end game for me.

I contacted the hospital and they advised me to take the medication, which I had with me. It was useless - the pain only got worse and worse. I thought I was going to explode! I decided to try and make my way to the hospital in Limerick more in hope than in confidence. Before I exited the hotel, I left a note at reception for the LDS team to apologise and explain that I had to take my leave because I needed to go to the hospital.

As I made my way home from Ennis, I contacted the hospital. They advised me not to go there until the morning clinics had commenced, as they would not be able to help me until then. I phoned Mary, told her my story and that I was on the road home. She confided to me later that she was convinced at that stage that the worst had now come to pass. Both of us admitted subsequently that we feared that this was the beginning of the end for me. As I left Ennis, I prayed to anybody in the Great Out There for help. I was willing to do deals with any deity that might listen to my call. In my condition, and going in the direction I thought I was heading, I didn't feel I was in a position to be choosy. For once, I hoped that I might meet a Gárda checkpoint where somebody might be able to help me, if only to think rationally as I was worried about my capacity to drive and the potential danger I might be to other road users. I had no such luck. The moon-washed streets of the town were empty and bare as was the road from Ennis all the way home to Limerick. Maybe it was just as well, because if I'd met the Gardaí, they might have thought that I was delirious and under the influence of something or other.

I gradually made my way homewards and the pain seemed to abate. By the time I got home, I was more or less recovered from whatever had assailed me in the dark of the Ennis night. As the morning passed, I recovered and decided to go back out to work in Ennis as I was told by the hospital that once the pain had gone, there was no need for me to go to the hospital. Consequently, I went out to Ennis and joined my colleagues for the day. In later times, they told me of their concerns when they read the note I'd left them explaining why I'd had to take my leave during the night, and their subsequent shock when they saw me arrive back to them later in the morning. For them, it must have been a sense of dead man walking...

I had my third cycle of chemotherapy at Halloween, which went very much according to plan. Professor Gupta was present at the Cancer Centre and told me that he was happy with the results of a CAT scan I had had the previous week. The scan showed that the chemotherapy was working. That was reassuring and made coping with the side-effects worthwhile. The positive feedback from Professor Gupta revitalised all of us and gave me the resolve to persevere, even when the going seemed all uphill. The fourth and fifth sessions of chemotherapy together with another CAT scan were all scheduled for the month of November. Although the CAT scan was a straightforward procedure, I found the liquid that I had to drink in preparation for it most unpleasant. It was literally a case of having to hold your nose and swallow your medicine.

I had to travel from a team meeting in Athlone in November to a meeting in Dublin that night, when the Dublin to Galway motorway was still under construction. The slow-moving evening traffic approaching the town of Moate presented me with an understanding as to a possible origin of the expression, "You scratch my back and I will scratch yours". I observed two horses in a field standing side by side. Faced in opposite directions, they were oblivious to the passing traffic while they combed each other's backs with their teeth. The kind and reciprocating nature of the horses led me to imagine that the expression might well have its origins in the animal world. Whether my theory was well founded or not the horse cameo raised my spirits above the cares of the world.

The rigors often visited me at the most inopportune moments. As I reached my destination in Dublin, they struck me with full force while I was parking the car at my destination. I got out of the car and grabbed the side of it with one hand in an effort to control my body – I was shaking like somebody having a seizure while I fumbled in my pocket, searching for medication in the hope that it might bring some relief. At times like this, the rigors were so strong that not even morphine brought relief. Any innocent observer in the car park that night would have concluded that I was an addict who needed a fix. When the worst had passed, I went into the hotel to check in, and on the wall behind the receptionist was a Rodney Atkins quote; "If you're going through hell, keep on going, don't slow down." I felt as if somebody had been reading my diary.

I joined the meeting as scheduled and it was business as usual. That was the only way to play it. I constantly motivated myself to persevere by telling myself, "Wilt and there will be no turning back." It's like when a runner stops running in a race – it's very difficult to get back into a sound rhythm again. My attitude was to keep the head down like an armadillo and hope that nobody noticed. In retrospect, I know that dealing with particular side effects as I did with the rigors enabled me to convince myself that I had some control of the situation, or even that I was winning my battle with cancer. The rigors began with a bout of nausea and culminated with quite severe pain and shaking. To date, six years later, I still get minor versions of them that involve a sudden bout of nausea followed by a tremor through the body without the pain. I used to call them aftershocks until the natural disasters in Haiti, Christchurch and Japan. Now, I prefer to call them flashes from the past.

I had my final session of the autumn course of chemotherapy in the first week of December. Professor Gupta met me and was in a very positive frame of mind. After that, I had another CAT scan. That signalled the end of the autumn course of treatment and the beginning of the next phase of the journey. I had worked hard with my positive thinking, self-talk, visualisation and meditation exercises, in which I focused on pushing the cancer out of my body. The medical team arranged that I would meet with the Cancer Centre psychologist to discuss the strategies I was employing. My first reaction to the invitation to meet with the psychologist was that the medical team might not be comfortable with what I was doing, or worse still, that they might have concerns with regard to my mental health given the nature of some of the exercises I used.

I was pleasantly relieved when the psychologist assured me that it was part of their work as my care team and that they were very interested in the positive manner in which I appeared to be coping. Her complimentary remarks reminded me of a song, *The Great Pretender* written by Buck Ram and sung by Roy Orbison among others, especially the lines:

> *"Oh yes, I'm the great pretender*
> *Pretending that I'm doing well*
> *My need is such, I pretend too much*
> *I'm lonely but no one can tell"*

"Oh yes, I'm the great pretender

Adrift in a world of my own"

I had three meetings with the psychologist, the first of which was at Halloween, another in November and the third in December. I was encouraged at the first two meetings to continue with the approach that I was employing because the exercises seemed to be enabling and sustaining me in the journey.

I had noticed during November that I was getting progressively weaker. I found that carrying loaded bags of any description demanded great effort and even distressed me from time to time. I would have to leave down anything I was carrying for any distance and rest before continuing. I was not traumatised by this occurrence, it just meant that I had to plan and do things differently. I also noticed that the sole of my left foot got sore whenever I walked a few hundred yards. I convinced myself that the soreness was caused by my visualisation routines, one of which involved opening the room window and imagining that I pushed the cancer down my body and out through the soles of my feet, from where it was driven out through the open window. Outside, it was blown into the atmosphere where it was burned by the heat of the sun and the cleansing rays from the heavens. I believed that it was important to have the window open to release the cancer to be burned; otherwise it could cling onto another person in whom it might secure residence. I did not want to send it out of my body and into another person or creature. The cancer had to be destroyed and this was my way of coping with it. Whether I was crazy or otherwise didn't really come into it. I did what I needed to do to sustain myself and protect others from the evil illness.

I had an ECG, a chest x-ray and a pulmonary breathing test in the run up to Christmas in preparation for high-dose chemotherapy and the stem cell transplant scheduled for early January. I was found to be in fit condition for the treatment ahead and I was fitted with a Hickman line on 22nd December, through which the chemotherapy, stem cell transplant and any other treatments would be infused. I remember the doctor telling me the pros and cons of fitting it. I didn't want to hear what could go wrong when fitting it and eventually, I asked him what his success rate was in this procedure. His answer was one hundred per cent. I assured him that I had no reason to doubt his competence and told him that without it, my chances were greatly reduced. I remember telling him that his success record with the procedure was more than adequate for me. I knew he had to follow protocol and respected his attention to detail in this regard. He was a professional with a hundred per cent success record - what more could anyone offer a patient? It was time to get the job done and he did.

The chemotherapy took its toll. I grew bloated and lost all my body hair. The left side of my body was in bad shape. There were days when my left foot was so painful that I could scarcely use it. The side effects hit with no mercy. I was in the closing rounds of a dogfight; nevertheless I was determined to fight on. I did not want sympathy. I wanted remission. I was quickly running out of options. I was haunted by Joe Louis's immortal words to Billy Conn on the eve of their world heavyweight title fight (17th June, 1941), "You can run but you can't hide!" There was no place to hide. Hunter Thompson said, "You can turn your back on a person, but never turn your back on a drug, especially when it's waving a razor sharp hunting knife in your eye." I could turn my back on many things in life and walk away, but there was no way that I could turn my back on cancer because it is like an angel of death for those it strikes; seeking, finding, wearing down and finally taking.

CHAPTER EIGHT

Life on the Outside

"When the world says, 'Give up,' Hope whispers, 'Try it one more time."

- Author Unknown

Richard Power, Gerry Berkery and Michael O'Brien were always at hand when needed to drop me out to the hospital in the mornings for treatment, and Mary would collect me after she finished school. There were many things people did to help. Phone calls and text messages were always welcome, especially when spirits were low or the challenge seemed insurmountable. On the days I had chemotherapy, text messages wishing me the best of luck would begin to arrive from around 8 a.m. and would continue right through the day. I was always assured of many texts as I made the short but lonesome walk from the car park into the Cancer Centre. The kindness and generosity of people knew no bounds. Friends and neighbours extended offers from walking the dog to doing our laundry. Fortunately, we did not have to call in the offers. Added to this, Edel O'Doherty gave me an angel worry box containing three angels to take care of me. They are treasured keepsakes and I still call upon them when times get tough.

I was very touched when a young man who did his teaching practice some years previously in the school where I worked phoned me to wish me well. His thoughtfulness and the kind contact from so many people made me think I must have done something good for someone along the way. They made me feel that I had a life worth fighting for.

I got mass bouquets, relics and holy medals, together with get well cards from many people. I was grateful to everyone who sent me messages of goodwill. I was particularly taken by the number of cards and messages of support I received from the people of my native West Clare. This support immediately tugged at my heart. It brought tears, not of pain but of raw emotion. These people actually cared enough for me and my family in our time of need. I believe that all of this sustained us. However, there was a flipside to this experience - I did not hear from some people whom I had hoped would make contact.

"Faithless is he that says farewell when the road darkens"
- J.R.R. Tolkien

Goodwill came to us in many forms and gave us the energy to carry on. Equally, the divine powers people called upon, especially Padre Pio and St. Matthew, to intervene on my behalf delivered results in due course. I felt a noticeable turn for the better in my battle with cancer around a time that I received Padre Pio and St. Matthew relics and oils from friends. Although I am not one to go on pilgrimages, I have always respected every person's religious beliefs and practices.

I believe that spirituality is a personal thing and everyone should be allowed to practice as they choose. The rosary was a central part of family life when my generation was growing up. I put my faith in it. Paradoxically, I was determined that I would not be ambushed by any God squad or some group of self-appointed apostles who might want to put my cry for pity on their bill board. Neither was I inclined towards investing in shares in the afterlife just yet because I did not want to go there. I was prepared to pass on the one-way ticket that would take me to that better place on the other side, regardless of how good the facilities there might be. If deals could be done, I wanted a stay of execution on the sentence placed upon me. The better place for me was at home with my family. Towards this outcome, I welcomed everything that came my way, from the lighting of a penny candle to intercessions with whatever greater powers people believed in. I still have a small stone in a jacket pocket that a pilgrim from West Clare brought back for me from Croagh Patrick. I would never dismiss help from any quarter, especially not when it seemed as if the compass of my future was pointing towards very disturbed waters.

A family friend from my native West Clare, Mary Quinlan, passed away at the end of September, 2005, and I was unable to get to the funeral because of my hospital commitments. Equally, I was not in a proper emotional state to attend a funeral in the circumstances. I phoned her brother, Joe Quinlan, who was a great neighbour to my family for many years, to extend my sympathies on the occasion of Mary's death. While he appreciated the sentiment of my call, he quickly focused on my predicament and gave me a motivationally inspiring pep talk. He told me that I needed to focus on my battle with cancer. He impressed on me that I owed it to my family and myself to dig deep for one almighty effort. He assured me that I had what it took to fight now and beat the cancer. I will always remember him for the manner in which he put aside his grief for his sister to lend words of encouragement to me. When I was growing up at home, Joe and his late brother John, who passed away in June 2012, were the neighbours we called on when we needed a helping hand. They were our emergency response team when life's crises struck. Joe was at hand once again when I needed him.

The fight was on, the stakes were high and it was a case of life or death. This was a surreal experience. It was my life and I felt like someone outside looking in on it. I never felt more like somebody on stage. The following lines from William Shakespeare's, *All the World's a Stage* rang true as I struggled on, fearing my exit and playing many parts I never imagined.

> *"All the world's a stage,*
> *And all the men and women merely players;*
> *They have their exits and their entrances,*
> *And one man in his time plays many parts…"*

While all of this went on in our own home, I did my best to keep my mother calm and visit her every fortnight. I was neither a martyr nor a victim. In fact I was very much pampered by many who went out of their way to support me. Everybody focused on me, the patient. I often felt that Mary, Brian and Ronan were the victims in the situation and as such, suffered most. Their emotions and needs went unattended and even neglected. I felt so angry at the loss of my health and the agony and pain it brought on my family and those close to me.

Christmas 2005 – My mother (Annie Haugh) and I.

On the work scene, I was delighted to finalise an arrangement with DELL Computers for the provision of computers for the school in October. A representative informed me that the company would donate thirty desktop computers to the school to equip a computer room, plus supplementary hardware for classroom use. This put the school on a good footing to meet the IT learning needs of the children and adult learners in the community. Equally, it was gratifying to deliver on what had been considered a somewhat lofty IT ambition of mine for the school. It was a good day's work and I savoured the feel-good factor that went with closing the deal. It was particularly pleasing to be able to deliver for the school community on this occasion because although I was away on secondment, its wellbeing was still very important to me.

Brian moved into his new house on Friday, 16th December, and Ronan spent some time helping him to get settled in. The following day, Mary and I went to town to do some Christmas shopping. It was quite a treat to soak up some of the Christmas atmosphere and even indulge ourselves with a coffee, together with something savoury to the palate and sinful to the waistline. I happened to meet some past pupils in Cruises Street; the first had become a post-primary teacher and the second was plying a trade I had taught him in school; he was busking on a tin whistle playing Christmas carols to the delight of his captive audience, as well as treating them to recitations from his second collection of poetry. I met a few more from yesteryear and we reminisced about times gone by. I got great satisfaction from hearing their success stories. It was wonderful to know that they had become responsible citizens with their own homes and were living happy lives with their partners and families. "They came from good homes", I told myself. I remembered their parents with great admiration. I also hoped that the much-maligned education system might have done something right somewhere along the way. Regardless, it was a good day and we enjoyed the festive goodwill that radiated from the people we met. Their kindness and goodwill were balm to the soul on that day.

We decided that we would celebrate Christmas. We would adhere to the usual norms of the festive season. There was no hiding the reality of my illness, especially now that my physical appearance had changed so much that people only recognised me by the sound of my voice when I spoke. Mary and the boys had the house decorated splendidly for the festive season. I was very aware that my mother, Annie, was in a very emotional state so we decided to do what we could to keep a positive mood about the house. I took her to shopping centres in an effort to generate some festive spirit for her. Mary, Brian and Ronan did more than their fair share to keep things positive and lived in the present. In hindsight, we all probably did quite well on that score. There was also the haunting fear in my mind: "Would this be my last Christmas?" Christmas vigil mass was an emotional event, compounded by the fact that people did not recognise me. I found that truly scary. We exchanged Christmas presents and we passed Christmas Day with our usual Christmas rituals.

An appointment with Professor Gupta on 29th December to finalise arrangements in advance of the high-dose chemotherapy and the stem cell transplant brought a reality check. There was no respite from cancer, not even during the season of goodwill. He went over the entire procedure - the transplant and the aftercare - with us and answered any questions we had. We knew that personal hygiene would be crucial, together with avoiding situations in which I could pick up infections when I left the hospital. He told us that our dog, Buddy, would not pose a health risk to me. We were very, very relieved because we had visions of having to move the poor creature out of our home, which would have traumatised him immeasurably.

The old year drew to a close. This time we did not have the heart to ring out the old year and ring in the new one as we had done for more than twenty years with our close friends Richard and Marie Power. In truth, there was nothing to celebrate and there was no point in trying to delude ourselves. The Powers understood as only good friends would and could.

Mary and I took Buddy to Beale Beach in Kerry to celebrate New Year's Day. We needed to get out of the house to avoid an onset of the blues, which can easily creep up on one living under the shadow of cancer. It was a great escape from the confinement of the house. We had miles of beach, seabirds, fresh air and the rolling tide to refresh our minds. Buddy enjoyed the freedom of the open space, the sand and simply running free. We walked on the beach to the sound of the waves breaking on the seashore and the lonely cry of the seagulls until evening began to close in on us. I told myself that there would be more days like this. However, when it was time to leave, I cast a long, last lingering look across the River Shannon at my beloved West Clare where the sun was setting; a place where I spent a happy and carefree childhood. As the fading sunlight gradually made way for the cloak of night, I gazed over at the fading shoreline, choking back the tears, wondering if I would survive the cancer and go there again, or if it would be left to my spirit to join my Celtic ancestors in that land of gentle breezes and peaceful waters. I could never have imagined that I would have an experience like this, not even in my worst nightmares. Despite my best efforts to hold them back, the tears began to escape, slowly at first until they burst forth and raged like a storm of wind and rain. It was time to go home. I took one last gasp of sea air and left the rest to destiny. We left in a deafening silence as the clouds of night rolled in.

When we got home, I fumbled about trying to pass the time. True to form, we had a most welcome visit from Richard and Marie Power, who stayed with us late into the night. It was a difficult and emotional time when we bade them goodnight.

We spent the time playing down the clock to HD-day, that is, when high-dose chemotherapy would commence. I had telephone calls from many people wishing me the best of luck in the days and weeks ahead. I had a call from Michael Troy, a man for whom I had the greatest respect and admiration when

I was growing up in West Clare, and I still hold him in highest esteem. He was an outstanding footballer and I had the privilege of playing with him for a number of years. It was great to hear from somebody I considered a role model when I was growing up.

On the 3rd January, there was an air of apprehension about the house. The waiting was nearly over. It was as if the inevitable was approaching in the darkness and none of us had any control. It reminded me of Seán Ó Riordáin's imagery in *Oíche Nollag na mBan* when he talks of the silence coming to consume him in the darkness. There was a sense of helplessness, hopelessness, anger, fear, anguish, desperation and claustrophobia. The lines from Shakespeare's *King Lear,* which I'd learned reluctantly for my Leaving Cert in the early seventies, came to mind. I hoped that Lear's mental condition was not about to befall me:

"Blow, winds, and crack your cheeks! rage! blow!
You cataracts and hurricanes, spout
Till you have drench'd our steeples, drown'd the cocks!
You sulphurous and thought-executing fires,

Vaunt-couriers to oak-cleaving thunderbolts,
Singe my white head! And thou, all-shaking thunder,
Strike flat the thick rotundity o' the world!
Crack nature's moulds, all germens spill at once
That make ingrateful man!"

We are told that there is a silver lining behind every cloud, as there was for Lear - he recovered. I lived in hope that a positive outcome was in store for me in the days, weeks and even months ahead.

Much as I focused on a positive outcome, there was always a risk of the unthinkable. It was like looking in on our lives from the outside. It is impossible to describe. There was no roller coaster of emotions now. Our hearts were heavy and although we were clockwatching, nobody mentioned tomorrow. It felt like something painful was gnawing mercilessly at us and it would never give up! By nightfall, the volcano of emotions erupted and overflowed. Even Buddy the dog put on his caring hat when he sensed the mood of desperation and fear. He had a propensity to sense when emotions were raw or at low ebb. Whenever he noticed our spirits were plummeting, he would rest his head on our feet or sit beside us and put his chin on our lap and look up at us with sadness in his eyes as if to say, "I know you are feeling down, but trust me, things will get better." Despite Buddy's finest therapy skills, none of us wanted the night to end because we dreaded what the next day would bring. The time had come for me to swallow my fear, meet my destiny and play my last ace.

CHAPTER NINE

Navigating Perilous Waters

"Feel the fear and do it anyway,"

- Susan Jeffers (1988)

On Wednesday, 4th January, it was a case of walking the walk with regard to Susan Jeffers's mantra, "Feel the fear and do it anyway!" The preparation had been carried out meticulously by Professor Gupta and his team. I was as mentally focused as I felt I could be, in the awareness that this would be the toughest undertaking of my life to date. I had to believe that I was up to the task ahead and whatever it would demand of me. I knew that I was in poor physical shape so I hoped that I might summon the mental and emotional strength to see me through the challenges that lay in store for me. I wasn't thinking any further ahead than days. The days would then grow into weeks.

I dragged myself out of bed and went to the hospital for blood tests, after which I was allowed home until noon. I would be admitted then for treatment, provided the results of the blood tests were satisfactory. The uncertainty was nerve wracking. We passed the time with a mid-morning meal before setting out again for the hospital at noon. Conversation was strained as the time to leave home approached. Then it was time to bite the bullet and be on our way. I settled into my room, which would be my prime area of residence for the next three to four weeks. I assured myself that I was not there for the hospitality or the view from the room window. I was there for an almighty onslaught on the cancer, which I saw as a parasite that was refusing to vacate my body. I prepared myself mentally, seeing the chemotherapy as heavy artillery that would attack the enemy from all quarters, bombarding the cancer with high-dose treatment twice daily. I resolved to be patient. I would call on myself and summon all my inner strength. Each part of the treatment would do its work; I had to do my part. If the going got tough, then I had to be tougher. Nothing lasts forever. I told myself that there was one great fight somewhere in me; I believed I was up to it. I found meaning in the words of the great Mahatma Gandhi, "You can chain me, you can torture me, you can even destroy this body, but you will never imprison my mind."

The first session of chemotherapy started soon after I was admitted. Professor Gupta dropped in to see me and check that all was going according to schedule. He told me that I could go home between the morning and night treatments for a break. Infusion of chemotherapy took about four hours so I was let home at about 5.30 p.m. where I had my tea and relaxed before returning to the hospital around 9 p.m. as scheduled. I settled in for the night and infusion of chemotherapy commenced in due course. I passed the time returning phone calls and psyching myself to fight the cancer. It was late into the night before the procedure was completed. Afterwards, I had to attend to the hygiene rituals before embarking on my final lot of visualisation exercises. The day was an oxymoron for me - I did not want to be in hospital but I wanted to get on with the treatment.

The next three days followed a pattern. Infusion of chemotherapy began at around 10 a.m. and lasted until about 12.30 p.m., after which I was allowed to go home. I returned to the hospital after 8 p.m. and the second session of chemotherapy commenced at about 10 p.m. I also had to put drops into my eyes every three hours, day and night, so I set an alarm on my phone to make sure that I managed that. I was very aware that I had to be vigilant with regard to every aspect of the treatment and failure to do so would have adverse consequences for me. The medical team was the epitome of professionalism and kindness in every respect. Mary, Ronan and Brian were doing their best to keep positive. Ronan was trying to balance the challenges of my sickness with preparations for his first set of exams in UL, which were scheduled to begin on 10th January. Not an easy task to undertake. Life goes on and so it did - he was just a number in college and had to do the best he could.

The 7th January was my mother's 85th birthday and I spoke to her on a number of occasions on the telephone in an effort to keep her in good spirits. In the course of our conversations, I realised that despite my best efforts to explain to her that the current course of treatment would take a few weeks at least, I got a sense that she was getting impatient and expected that it should be finished in a few days. I felt that maybe it was as well for her to think in that way or maybe it was just her way of coping with life's roulette. Who knows?

Time goes slowly when you're in hospital. However, Ciarán O'Neill, Charlie Morley and Michael Hanley did their best to keep me entertained with text messages by day and night. Text messages were wonderful in that they provided welcome light humour. I got phone calls, messages and more cards from past pupils, parents and people who had worked in the school in bygone days to wish me well in the fight. I welcomed every message and they sustained me when the going was tough.

On the fifth day of the course of chemotherapy, I realised that it was serious stuff. It was taking its toll on me physically, which in turn had an effect on my psychological attitude. I could feel myself slowing down. My blood pressure was low and consequently I needed an infusion of fluids to restore it to normal. The skin on my feet began to crack around my heels and they required regular applications of ointment. I was gradually beginning to fall apart like a battered ship in a storm. Metaphorically, I had to baton down the hatches and ride out the storm. I was in safe hands with a captain like Professor Gupta at the helm, ably assisted by a crew of competent medics.

The mental warfare went on unabated. The gremlins came at me in the dark of night. They lurked in the shadows waiting until I was alone. Then they tormented me whenever my defences were wavering, especially when the chemotherapy and the cancer seemed to be raging in battle. They would mock me and sneer at me. They were like demons in the dark, audible to my ears only. It was not a time to be faint hearted. I resolved to be ruthless in my physical battle with cancer and my psychological warfare with whatever gremlins presented themselves to break my resolve and endurance. There was only one option and that was to stand up and fight my way out of the situation. Sleep was always a welcome respite.

Day six of high-dose chemotherapy dawned and I followed the routines of the previous days. In addition, there was a rigorous examination by the medical team to ensure that I was in a fit state for stem cell re-infusion, which was scheduled for the next day. While all was going according to plan, experience had taught me never to take anything for granted. Nothing was certain until tested, checked and rechecked. It was a busy day between sessions of chemotherapy and final preparation for the re-infusion, together with the logistics of travelling to Dublin. Eventually, the day came to a close and all of us repaired to our beds for the night. I cannot say that I slept well. I was torn between getting to sleep and topping up on positive thinking. I spent most of the night visualising myself walking away from the cancer and throwing it into incinerators, strategically located like litter bins along the route. There would be time enough for sleeping when the cancer was killed.

Mary and I left for Dublin by taxi, courtesy of the HSE, at 6 a.m. and we arrived at St. James's Hospital at around 9.30 a.m. where I was admitted around noon. The route to the ward from the admissions area was like a scene from a film. I had to go through a series of doors and hygiene rituals to combat any dangers of infection or contamination of the ward in which re-infusion would take place. Re-infusion commenced at 1.45 p.m. It was given through the Hickman line that had been inserted in my chest before Christmas. There were four bags and each took about fifteen minutes to infuse. Mary was allowed to stay with me during and after the procedure. It was great to have her company, especially in what was uncharted medical territory for both of us.

It was very difficult to believe that all of this was happening to me and to comprehend that I was as sick as the treatment I was receiving would suggest. There were times when I had almost to pinch myself and ask if I was watching a film or some programme on television. Somehow, whether it was arrogance, ignorance or downright stupidity on my part, I had never imagined that something like this could or would ever happen to me. Unfortunately, I now found myself in an unenviable position, and I had no option but to fight my way out of it.

It was not all about me. Life went on and Ronan was sitting his first set of exams in the University of Limerick. Exams are stressful at any time, not to mention poor Ronan having to cope with the additional uncertainty and stress of having me in hospital in Dublin. Brian had to get on with his work. All of us were well aware that life had to go on and that we had to muddle through this phase as best we could with as little fuss as possible, and hope that we did not draw any undue attention to ourselves or our circumstances. We certainly did not want to be victims. We wanted to bear our challenge in private with dignity. I was just one of the twenty-eight million people in the world suffering from cancer. Some were lucky in that they got remission from it, others were not so lucky. The prospect of remission kept us going.

I stayed in hospital overnight and Mary stayed in a hotel close by. The mobile phone networks must have made a fortune from the many, many people who kept in constant contact. The second phase of the re-infusion took place the next morning and thankfully, all went according to plan. We were scheduled to leave Dublin by ambulance at 2 p.m. However, we did not depart until 6 p.m. When we arrived at the hospital, we got the pleasant news that I was allowed home for the night. We got a fabulous welcome from Ronan, Brian and Buddy. That night, the Irish proverb "Níl aon tinteáin mar do thinteáin féin" (there is no hearth like your own hearth) had more meaning than I'd ever imagined. It was great to be home.

The next morning, I got a terrible shock when I looked in the mirror and saw what I could not believe was my own reflection. I didn't recognise the man in the mirror looking out at me. Suddenly, my body had become so much more bloated and my face was really puffed. Now, I really was a mere shadow of my former self. Well, the neighbours did not recognise me at Christmas, and here I am now, unrecognisable to myself - what next? Better not go there, I told myself! It was time to be inspired by my own mantra to others when times are bad - Chin up, shoulders back, chest out and dress up! Mind you, dressing up on this occasion for me meant changing my pyjamas. The lines from Hunter Thompson's *Fear and Loathing in Las Vegas* came to mind, "There he goes. One of God's own prototypes. A high-powered mutant of some kind never even considered for mass production. Too weird to live, and too rare to die."

I felt very weak and my enthusiasm levels were low. Once again I had to dig deep into my reserve of human spirit; it was the only thing I could do. Even though I felt miserable and my life was balancing on a knife-edge, there was always hope, and I clung to it dearly. It was explained to me that the stem cell transplant had thrown my whole body out of sync in the same manner as an organ transplant would. Now, in a weird and unimaginable way, I was living on the precipice of my tenuous existence. I told myself that I was on the threshold of a great victory over cancer. My team and I had fought a long and hard battle over the last twelve months, and I was damned if I was going to throw in the towel at this stage. The darkest hour might be a long one, but we had to live in the hope of a brand new dawn. The odds had peaked and dipped for and against us over the past year. Now I was in the throes of battle looking the enemy straight in the eye with contempt and claiming back my health. With victory in sight, there was no alternative!

The next day was Friday, 13th January - not a day for the superstitious. Time goes slowly in hospital and today was no exception. I was lethargic and my concentration levels were low. It was difficult to motivate myself to get out of bed and wash. I felt like locking the door, curling up in the bed and closing myself off from all contact. However, the message kicked in that there was unfinished business - I had to get over the line and into recovery mode. Despite my poor energy levels, I pressed onwards.

The day improved when Professor Gupta and the medical team told me that they were very happy with my progress. They were also very pleased with the readings on my blood tests. All signs were positive, which lent assurance to all of us on the journey. Later that day I was told that I could go home for the weekend until Sunday, when I would have to return for blood tests. The thought of going home lifted my spirits immeasurably and it also reassured me that I must be on the mend if I was getting out of hospital, even if it was only temporarily. There is an old saying that one swallow doesn't make a summer, but at least it is a sign that summer is on its way. In like manner, getting out of hospital for a few days didn't mean that I was over the worst of my sickness, but at least it augured well!

On Saturday, the Munster rugby team provided the evening's entertainment on television when they overcame Castres. Munster played an outstanding game and their performance gave us all due reason to abandon our medical cares for the duration of the match and well into the night while we basked in the glory of their performance once again. It is a great old world and that is why I wanted to stay here!

The next morning I felt as if I was stuck to the bed. It took a great effort to get out of it and wash myself. I shuffled about the house and Buddy joined me for breakfast. Meanwhile, Mary had to take one of the cars to John and Kieran O'Donnell in Kildysart to have it serviced. This was a chore I always took care of and the banter with the O'Donnells was always enjoyable. Brian was on transport duty, ferrying Ronan to and from college for his exams. I felt fairly useless to the family in my role of spectator. I was like a grounded ship, incapacitated by my illness and there was no hiding from that reality. My independence was ripped from me and I was physically winged. However, I told myself that there were many times in the past when it might have been easier to opt out. I wanted to believe that capitulating under pressure was never my chosen option. I drew strength from the tough decisions I had taken in the past for the greater good when it might have been easier to take the more popular option. I had trudged on in marathons and got to the finishing line when my body told me that the tank was empty. Perseverance brought me through the state exams when I was in secondary school and I struggled to get my place on sports teams where others were an automatic choice. Life had taught me that some things in life are not impossible. It was simply that I had to try harder than my peers just to stay in the race. I found that the lessons I learned from enduring the trials and tribulations of the past sustained me when I had to search deep for the resources to keep going on this journey.

The taste of success was always my opium. Now, the reward for my endeavours was life itself. My will was constantly reassuring itself while my poor body was feeling the full impact of the cancer and the medication. I knew that success was somewhere in the Great Out There waiting for me to grasp it. Victory would require patience and perseverance, and I resolved that I would do my utmost to reclaim my health.

My body continued to get weaker and my energy levels dropped over the next three days as I went into survival mode. I was immersed in the routines of life in hospital. I felt like a junkie with all the medication I was taking. It was a full-time job attending to the various hygiene routines. I had very bad mouth sores and I decided in consultation with the medical team that I would get up regularly during the night and use the prescribed mouthwash to combat the damage that infections wreaked on me. While these demands kept me going at a great pace, blood tests and platelet counts were continually monitored because my white blood cells needed to drop to zero before I would go into recovery mode. Professor Gupta and the medical team assured me that all the signs were good in this regard and that my body was weakening so dramatically because of the white cell blood count dropping to zero. I realised that I was approaching a tightrope situation - when the white cells hit zero, I would have very little resistance if the pendulum of fate swung too far in the wrong direction!

The next day was Saturday and I was allowed to go home for the night. I had to return to the hospital the next morning for blood tests and an appointment with the medical team. They were happy with my physical and emotional wellbeing. My platelet levels were down to thirty-three, which was good, considering it was now twelve days since I'd begun high-dose chemotherapy. I was acutely aware that my body was now at an all-time low and very vulnerable to infection. I now needed to sustain myself with my mental strength. I had no idea what or where this journey would bring me. You could say I was drifting midstream and hoping that the compass was pointing forward. I had been lucky all my life and I believed that I had every reason to be optimistic, though cautious. It was now a case of *"Tread softly because you tread on my dreams,"* - W.B. Yeats.

On Sunday evening, I felt dreadful. I just felt like creeping into a corner and hiding there until whatever was happening to me had gone away. I decided that hospital was probably the best and only place for me. I remember saying to my family that I was going back into hospital that evening, and that I would stay there until I felt better. I empathised with our canine friends who choose solitude when they are feeling unwell. In a somewhat similar frame of mind, I silently went back to hospital to prepare for whatever measures were necessary to see me through the next phase of the process. In boxing terms, I was on the ropes. Now the time had come for me to punch above my weight, both mentally and physically. It wasn't going to be easy and I knew it. The struggle was not just mine. It upset Mary, Brian and Ronan together with my mother and close friends. I was very sick. I was also very angry because of all the upset those close to me had had to endure. I had turned into a human wreck.

Once again, I went through the usual nocturnal hygiene and medical rituals before retiring for the night. I got up at regular intervals to attend to mouth-washing in an effort to curb the infections that were a side effect of the treatment. The next morning, my haemoglobin was still over ten and my white cell count was 0.03. So near and yet so far from the required 0.00 before recovery could begin. The medical team spared no effort with their care. There was a *"No Visitors"* sign on my door because my resistance to infections was low and every precaution had to be taken to reduce the risk of infection. I would later refer to this period as "the lock-in".

Around this time there was a lot of difficulty over a shortage of beds and patients were put on trolleys along the corridors. One night I overheard a heated discussion in which the nurse in charge stood firm to prevent patients from being put on trolleys in the corridors of the ward. When I enquired how they would manage for bathroom facilities, I was informed that in such circumstances, patients were given bed-pans. I wondered whether the germs whose presence was facilitated by such toilet arrangements were able to read the *"No visitors"* sign on the door of my ward. Would they adhere to the health and safety protocols?

Right around this time, the Celtic tiger economy was the envy of the world and here we were in Limerick with medical staff struggling to find accommodation for patients in corridors, on trolleys with bed-pans, while those who had the power to help turned a blind eye. It was an insult to medical staff and inhumane treatment of the sick and dying.

I was very upset when I heard that John McNamara from Tarmon in West Clare died on 16th January. He had been suffering from cancer. John played football with me for St. Cronan's GAA Club in West Clare in the 1970s. He was a great marksman and our top scorer in 1976 when we won the County Junior Championship. He was the hero of the replayed final against Kilfenora when he scored the all-important goal that set the game alight and put us on the road to victory. He was an absolute gentleman and he would be missed.

I felt like I was in the latter stages of a marathon race with my body telling me it had had enough and that it was exhausted. I had to ask it for one more effort to run off the pain in the belief that together, my body and I could overcome the fatigue and the aches. It was squeezing just that little bit extra out of it to get over the finish line. The finishing time becomes irrelevant when the wheels come off and you are having a bad run. All you want to do is complete the course. You do not want to drop out. Some might say it is vanity or plain stubbornness that keeps you going, but the feeling of overcoming a challenge against the odds is personal and inexplicable. You have to feel the experience to understand. The situation in which I now found myself reminded me of Richard Power's philosophy when matters are not going according to plan in a marathon. Sometimes you have to forget about doing a good time. The challenge becomes more like show jumping - you forget about the clock and go for a clear round. I wanted a clear round on this occasion. For once in my life, time was neither a priority nor an issue.

CHAPTER TEN

An Báidóir Uaigneach - The Lonesome Boatman

"I know God will not give me anything I can't handle. I just wish that He didn't trust me so much."

- Mother Teresa

The next week would prove vital. On Tuesday, I felt as though I was watching ER on television when I had two bags of platelets and three units of blood infused. I got a bout of shivers near the end of the third unit of blood. I learned that it was all part of the process but unnerving. When it happened, I hit somewhere between serious concern and panic as once again I wondered if this was some sort of termination alarm. Obviously, the shivers passed, another event to add to the growing list of experiences in my encounter with cancer. None of them pleasant, and nothing that I would recommend, not even to pass a wet month on holidays.

I had to remind myself that all of this was a small price to pay and that I was luckier than most with an ultimate outcome well worth fighting for. I had to be patient and mindful that my journey would be slow, tedious and uncertain. I allowed myself to be inspired by the philosophy of the Irish proverb, "De réir a chéile a thógtar na caisleáin"- Castles are built gradually, and I was prepared to give whatever might be required of me both in time and in effort.

Mary and Ronan called to see me that evening. Brian collected Ronan but could not drop in to see me because he'd had a tummy bug a few days earlier. The next day I was really sick. My mouth was on fire and I tried to cool it with copious supplies of water. I made frequent and hurried visits to the bathroom. This was becoming part of my new lifestyle. I did the best I could to compose myself and play down the frequency, just as teams play down the clock in sport. However, this was neither entertaining nor sport. The doctors had told me that there would be days like this. I had to brace myself, navigate the disorder, take each challenge as it presented itself and forget about it once it had passed. I was not going to complain. I needed to toughen up and get over it. I was not going to play the sympathy card and cause my family further concern. I felt that they were already overburdened without my adding to their agony. What purpose would that serve? I resolved to keep as upbeat as possible for their sakes and anyway, if I dropped into a pit of negativity, it would be all the more difficult to climb out of it. Life and literature had taught me not to make any pronouncements in exasperation. Oscar Wilde once commented on the wallpaper in his bedroom during his twilight days - "Either it goes or I go." Unfortunately for him, he went!

Professor Gupta called to see me in the afternoon, by which time I was washed and out of bed, which must have been a good sign. He discussed my situation with me and answered whatever questions I had. He assured me that he was happy with how matters were progressing, and that raised my spirits immeasurably. If he was happy today, I had every reason to be equally happy and optimistic because he would not give me false hope. Every day was a bonus, and the longer I stayed on course, the better. It was rather like the travellers' strategy for coping with a runaway horse, "Stay, stay 'wi' her boy, stay 'wi' her and she'll tire." I just had to hang in there, and "stay 'wi' her and hope she'll tire."

Over the next five days, I scrambled and fumbled as my energy levels were very low. I knew I was in bad shape. Every passing day, I had to dig deeper into whatever reserves I had to keep going. It was draining emotionally and physically; there was no shortcut, no place to hide and no room for self-pity. This was a fight for survival. It was like a bullfight - one of us would come out of it alive; it would be the cancer or me, simple as that! I was cornered and I had to be vigilant for my own survival. I was very, very angry and at the same time, afraid to fall asleep because I feared that I might not wake up again. I hated being alone and I dreaded the darkness of night. I was a prisoner of fear. Terrified of dying, ceasing to be. Gone just like leaves on the trees when winter begins or a candle blown out in the wind. The prospect of the long cold sleep and eternal silence chilled me.

The truism of Isaac Asimov's words "Life is pleasant. Death is peaceful. It's the transition that's troublesome." haunted and tormented me night and day, but I kept my fears to myself. There was no point burdening anyone else. I remember bursting out crying once in Mary's presence and felt so very ashamed of myself for offloading my fears on her. She had enough to contend with. Still, she never complained. I also felt particularly ashamed of one occasion when she called to see me after her day's work and I drifted off to sleep in her presence. Needless to say, she did not complain and went to great lengths to tell me that I just needed to rest. That's Mary; patient, understanding and enduring at all times.

On Thursday, 19th January, I developed some sort of an infection that had to be treated with an intravenous antibiotic. When the antibiotic was infused on Friday, it was followed by two lots of platelets and I was feeling the worse for wear when Ronan arrived to lift my spirits. He regaled me with his stories in his usual humorous manner. The challenges the public bus service presented in no way dented either his obvious delight and relief to be finished his exams and his intent to raise my spirits. He was looking forward to the holidays and a good rest, punctuated with regular celebratory outings.

I got up several times during that night to wash out my mouth in the hope that it would help banish the infection I had. My efforts were rewarded in that I was able to eat a bowl of cereal and have a cup of tea for breakfast. This was a major breakthrough. I must have turned my celebration breakfast of cereal into a banquet because I hadn't time to wash myself before I was hooked up to a drip. This was followed by a transfusion of two lots of platelets and a unit of blood. It struck me that this was indeed a change of fortune. Two years previously on 20th January 2004, I'd had the honour of welcoming then President Mary McAleese to Galvone N.S. where I was principal. I could never have imagined then that two years later, I would have spent more than a year fighting a losing battle with cancer. Cancer was destroying me. It had reduced me to a state of physical wreckage. Cancer never sleeps; I was too frightened to sleep and too weary to cry. Long-term did not exist. There was only the present. Surviving each moment and staying alive was my consuming mission. The words of Robert William Service's poem, *The Quitter*, resonated particularly with me:

When you're lost in the Wild, and you're scared as a child,

And Death looks you bang in the eye,

And you're sore as a boil, it's according to Hoyle

To cock your revolver and . . . die.

But the Code of a Man says: "Fight all you can,"

And self-dissolution is barred.

In hunger and woe, oh, it's easy to blow . . .

It's the hell-served-for-breakfast that's hard.

"You're sick of the game!" Well, now, that's a shame.

You're young and you're brave and you're bright.

"You've had a raw deal!" I know -- but don't squeal,

Buck up, do your damnedest, and fight.

It's the plugging away that will win you the day,

So don't be a piker, old pard!

Just draw on your grit; it's so easy to quit:

It's the keeping-your-chin-up that's hard.

It's easy to cry that you're beaten -- and die;

It's easy to crawfish and crawl;

But to fight and to fight when hope's out of sight --

Why, that's the best game of them all!

And though you come out of each gruelling bout,

All broken and beaten and scarred,

Just have one more try -- it's dead easy to die,

It's the keeping-on-living that's hard.

On Saturday 21st January, while the Munster rugby team played Sale Sharks, I was having a transfusion of blood and platelets. Mary kept me company all day, for this, my second round of transfusions in a week. Meanwhile, our Munster heroes delivered an emphatic win with a score of 31 points to 9. David Wallace finished the game with another of his signature tries. Our cheering must have been heard throughout the corridors of the hospital because I have great admiration for David, especially as he had given generously of his time by visiting the school to meet the children, sign autographs and pose for photos after he toured with the British and Irish Lions Rugby Team in 2001.

The school made a presentation to him to mark his selection as a British and Irish Rugby Lion, and a plaque was unveiled on the *Wall of Fame* in the school in honour of the occasion. The teachers, especially the female ones, were as pleased and excited as the children, if not more so, to meet him and have photos taken with him! I thanked heavens for Mary's company and support on that day and also David Wallace and the Munster Rugby Team for delivering another of their classic performances. They raised my spirits when they most needed raising. Equally, I give thanks to the blood donors who give their blood so generously for people like me and others who need transfusions. Without such acts of kindness of spirit, I would not be alive today, which is a sobering and chastening thought!

Sunday arrived. I felt terrible as I shuffled about the ward like a drunk on his way home in the dark after closing time. I made the decision to be as upbeat as possible because I believed that life was difficult enough on Mary, Brian, Ronan and my mother, together with others close to me. I told myself to toughen up and be grateful that I was still alive, that the medical team seemed pleased with the rate of progress, and that it was a matter of doing as I was told (many might say that was a first for me!). I was determined to weather the storm. I needed to revise my opinion on the existence of the long-term. I needed to refocus and take encouragement from the philosophy of Charles C. Noel, "*You must have long-range goals to keep you from being frustrated by short-range failures.*"

To this end, I decided that I would make my nightly circuits of the hospital corridor count towards rebuilding myself with the goal of participating in the transplant games for athletes who, as the name suggests, have undergone transplant operations. The psychological boost was immense as the thought of running again and the prospect of a return to physical activity sent surges of adrenalin through my dilapidated body. Immediately, I got on the phone to Mary to let her know about my plans. They were most definitely plans and not ambitions. I was in no mood for anything other than concrete plans. I commissioned Mary, together with Ronan and Brian, to source all the information they could on the transplant games from the internet. Once I was armed with the information, I could put my training plan in place for the hospital corridor.

I was never a great athlete or footballer of any sort, but all my life I'd used sport to keep myself in reasonably good physical condition and gained some degree of mental strength from my efforts. This stood me in good stead in my circuit training on the hospital corridor every night when all was quiet. The doctors had set me a target of walking about 25 metres to the end of the corridor and back at least once every night. I pushed myself from doing three circuits per night to walking twelve circuits. There were times when I shed tears of anger and desperation as I struggled to get every last step out of myself. Cancer was my adversary and here we were like two players marking each other on the playing pitch, even if that pitch was the corridors of the hospital. This was man-to-man marking as I had never experienced or imagined in my wildest dreams. There was no margin for error. I had to keep my opponent scoreless at all costs.

Walking close to the wall reminded me of the infamous wall ass that gets its name from walking close to a wall so that it might drag its burden or mount against the rough surface with a view to offloading it. In many ways I was like the wall ass, hoping to offload my burden with the aid of the wall and whatever other supports I might source to enable me on my journey.

Once I'd set myself the goal of competing in the transplant games after I'd recovered, I transformed the circuits of the hospital corridor in my mind into circuits of the University of Limerick running track, where I imagined I was doing serious endurance training. I began to time myself for individual circuits of the hospital corridor as well as timing how long the full session took. It wasn't very long until I transformed the training ground in my mind into a full Olympic stadium where I competed with Team Ireland. Modesty forbids me to divulge how many gold medals I won! Each night came to a close when the nurses dropped off my nightcap. I then toasted the achievements of the day with the ghostly figure that looked out at me from the mirror on the wall. We never disagreed. The ghostly figure in the mirror repeated every word of my battle cry, "Take the fight to the enemy!"

To you, it might seem a crazy exercise of the mind, but for me, it made getting out of bed to train and compete for Team Ireland a much more inviting prospect than whinging and whining and cursing my luck. I did my fair share of cursing from time to time too, as anybody who knows me will verify. I am sure that the medical team were amused by my attitude as I shuffled along the corridor training for the transplant games. It must have looked like a scene from *One Flew Over The Cuckoo's Nest.*

When I got out of hospital and made enquiries about joining the transplant games community, I learned that I did not qualify because I did not have a transplant from a donor. My stem cells were harvested from me in September and transplanted back to me in January, therefore I did not qualify. The stem cells were my own. Those were the rules and I was not unduly upset about it. On the contrary, I was very grateful to the transplant games community for the motivation I got from the prospect of becoming part of their team. They gave me a goal when I needed it, and it served me very, very well.

Once I had refocused and pointed my psychological compass towards long-term goals, I was quickly brought back to dealing with the physical goals of manoeuvring between regular hygiene routines and bowel movements that struck like lightning. The demands of getting from my bed to the adjoining facilities reassured me that I still retained some semblance of athleticism. To compound matters, the inside of my mouth was covered with a fungus-like infection that would have made it the perfect setting for an anti-bacterial household detergent advertisement. It was an absolute mess in every respect despite my best efforts day and night to curb it with Difflam mouthwash. The doctor advised me to continue with the oral hygiene routines and he would monitor the situation.

A massive brown blister covered the sole of my left foot. Some would suggest that it was the result of the visualisation exercises I was now doing a number of times every day. It was the same process that I had been repeating for some months. I imagined pushing the cancer downwards through my body and out through the soles of my feet. Proponents of this theory would assert that it was more than a coincidence that the blister appeared on my left foot and that the cancer was located on the left side of my body. Whatever the true explanation, there were no arguments on the matter and everybody encouraged me to work even harder on the visualisation exercises. My efforts went from turbo-boost to rocket-charged.

I had a visit from Professor Gupta one morning. Even though it was Sunday, he was in the hospital visiting patients and in no hurry whatsoever. He assured me that he was very pleased with the progress I was making. He then told me that he would consider letting me home from hospital the following Thursday, 26th January. This was music to my ears in many ways. Suddenly, my mouth did not feel or look so bad and the journey to the adjoining facilities was of minor consequence. However, the encouraging news was tempered with caution, as he emphasised that there was still a long and demanding journey ahead for me. I had no reason to doubt him. The house rules in place while I was in hospital would be enforced at home too. I could not have any visitors, and hygiene rituals would have to be just as thorough. Mary dropped in to see me mid-morning and the news of my possible release from hospital in four days was a cause for optimism for us both and lifted our spirits immeasurably. The good news was a great source of relief to my mother when I phoned to tell her.

The following morning, the rituals and routines of hospital life started all over again. The predictable battles between mind and body continued. It felt that they were constantly screaming at each other. My body just wanted to creep into a corner and hope that everything would just go away. If only it were that easy. I found it difficult to believe that I had become so incapacitated. Regardless, I put everything aside to concentrate on coping by dealing with the moment and place I was in. There was no point indulging in self-pity.

Mary, Ronan and Brian called to see me when they had finished work and had had their dinner in the evening. They were in great form at the prospect of my going home in a few days. All three of them looked radiantly happy. It was quite some time since I'd seen them looking so happy. It was a moment we had only dared to dream of for quite some time. The war was not yet over against cancer, but somehow, the fact that I was to be allowed home from hospital augured favourably. Once again, it was a matter of waiting to see if the recent bombardment with high-dose chemotherapy had worked. We decided to be cautiously optimistic - we needed to go with the heart and travel on the wings of hope.

The realisation that I was going home materialised when the first of the nurses dropped in before she went home to say goodbye and wish me well, because I would be gone home by the time she returned later in the week. I thought it a very touching gesture on her part, and it also showed that there is a human as well as a professional side to the nursing profession, which is something that often goes unnoticed. As the week wore on, the nurses and ancillary staff called to say goodbye to me. It happened so often that I was beginning to wonder if they were relieved to be getting rid me! On a serious note, I was overwhelmed with their care and kindness, and flattered that they called to say goodbye and wish me well. In a way, it was a momentous occasion. I had been through a fairly serious procedure, I had come through it this far and the signs were favourable. All I had to do now was stay on course.

All my energy was now focussed on getting myself into the best possible shape for the road ahead. When the medical team called to see me on Tuesday morning, they were very happy with my condition. They told me that my bloods had recovered greatly and that there was a possibility that I might be allowed home the following day. Needless to say, I was delighted and texted almost everybody I knew to announce the good news. Going home was a great step forward.

Professor Gupta called to see me the next morning, Wednesday 25th January, and told me that I could go home. He spent quite some time briefing me on what I could expect in the days and weeks ahead. Great - at least he was talking about weeks, which augured well. He explained that I had just undergone a major transplant and that certain fall out was to be expected. He also warned me that I could expect a psychological low in about two weeks or so, and that it would be some time before I had a PET scan to establish whether the cancer was fully or partially cleared.

While I was excited at the prospect of getting home, I was very aware that the next few days and weeks would be vital. Nothing was certain. The future is always uncertain, but I had a greater appreciation now of how uncertain it really was! I would travel more in hope than confidence in the days, weeks and whatever time I had left ahead. It was out of my hands.

I snoozed through the day and around three o'clock, I shuffled about the ward and began preparing to go home. Everything took much longer now. I was moving almost in slow motion. It was not that I was taking my time; I simply couldn't go any faster. I tired quickly and had to stop every so often to rest. I had my bag packed, or perhaps it would be more accurate to say that I had everything thrown into a bag and ready to go when Mary called for me after she'd returned from work. I collected my prescriptions and certificates of illness for work before I said my last goodbyes to the staff. It was a powerful step in the battle against adversity and a major psychological victory, thanks to Professor Gupta, the medical team, and indeed to my family, friends and everyone who had supported me. It was time to move forward and face the future with caution.

Just out of hospital – Ronan, Mary and I celebrating Ronan's 18th Birthday – Jan 2006

CHAPTER ELEVEN

Blue Skies, Calmer Waters

"Never deprive someone of hope; it might be all they have."

- H. Jackson Brown, Jr.

On the way home from the hospital, we collected the prescribed medication from our good friend and pharmacist, Michael Hanley. Michael came out to the car to say hello and wish me a continued recovery. It was probably the first occasion in years that the exchange between us was of such a sombre nature. I hoped that our days of banter and poking fun at each other would return again in the near future. And they did.

When I got home, I was greeted by Ronan, Brian and Buddy. Buddy was very excited to see me and the feeling was mutual. Once we'd had dinner, instead of relaxing I got busy organising our tax returns for the previous year, 2005. On reflection, my family must have had endless patience not to tell me to have sense because P60 forms would not be at hand for weeks or maybe months to come. Fortunately for them, I got tired after a while and had to concede that maybe it could wait until tomorrow. It was not very long until the rigours of the evening caught up with me and I went to bed soon after nine o'clock. I had convinced myself that the body had an opportunity to repair while I slept. It was great to be back in my own bed, despite the night sweats. I was in no hurry to get up the following morning until I eventually got out of bed around noon and took things easy. I had no choice in that because my energy levels were at an all-time low. A stranger looked out at me every time I passed the mirror. I got a bout of the shivers around evening time, which was another reminder that the cancer would not go away overnight. It was still raising a ruckus.

The challenge of living life with the uncertainty cancer brought me was never going to be easy. Now, waiting and watching over the next five or six weeks before I had a PET scan would prove another test of my endurance.

I spent the next weeks learning to cope with a series of highs and lows. There were times when I was manically happy to be alive and then there were other times when I was depressed, mourning the loss of my health and terrified that I would not get remission. The best high was being released from hospital and getting home to my family. It was great to be back in familiar surroundings, enjoying home foods and sleeping in my own bed. These are the things we take for granted until suddenly they are not there. Thankfully, my stay in hospital was only for a short period. The banter between Ronan and Brian at dinner was welcome. It wasn't long before they decided that they should resume their usual teasing about my many shortcomings, which really made me feel at home. It was good to know too that the lads were not treating me like some fragile ornament. It was wonderful to be home for Ronan's eighteenth birthday on the 30th January and my own birthday on 1st February. Ronan took me out for a few trips in the car while he practised his driving, and I was pleasantly surprised by the great improvement he demonstrated. I think he was relieved that I was complimentary of his driving as he'd endured some dreadful experiences with me a few months previously. I was the worst instructor poor Ronan could have had, and he bore the brunt of my shortfalls. Nevertheless, he persisted and now he was quite a competent driver.

I ventured out for a short walk on Sunday, 4th February to shake off the cabin fever that was beginning to set in. The world felt like a wonderful place as I experienced a series of resurrection moments from the people I met as I walked. The next day I took a longer walk and I felt like a politician on the election trail, saluting people and being greeted by everybody I met.

The rush of adrenalin caused me to walk until my feet got blistered. It was worth it though. I was out and about again, the feet would heal. Well, I hoped that they would, and they did, even if they took a little longer than they might have done before. My feet recovered in a few days, and I decided to build up my walking stamina and take Buddy with me. Taking Buddy with me turned out to be a dual purpose event. First, it gave him his daily walk, which was one less chore for Mary, and second, he was a great support as he walked timidly by my side until he noticed me tiring. Then he would walk slightly ahead of me, putting a slight pull on the lead until we reached home. He served me loyally for many weeks until I had recuperated a little. Once he felt that I had recovered enough strength and stamina, he reverted to his usual frolics - jumping and barking at cats at every given opportunity when we were on walkabouts.

Brian, Ronan and I on my 52nd birthday, February 1st 2006
– one week out of hospital.

Everything I did now was focused on rebuilding my mind and body, so I engaged in a three-way maintenance strategy. My primary focus was on eating healthily and prudently to ensure that my body got the food I needed to sustain my blood levels and to boost my immune system. Buddy was particularly partial to my culinary habits at lunchtime each day. Both of us ate well and consequently we put on excessive weight that demanded some serious walking when the summer months arrived.

I continued the mind games as a second maintenance strategy, and thirdly, I immersed myself in the labour of writing my memoir, together with a number of academic articles. Although the memoir is an unfinished work, parts of it proved enjoyable reading for Brian and Ronan as the recollections of my childhood gave them insights into a world that was very different to twenty-first century Ireland. The two lads were bemused to read that I went to a one-teacher school where we had dry toilets, no running water and a turf fire that we (the pupils) lit every morning in wintertime. When they read that we did not have electricity in the school either, they quipped, "Sure we always knew that you came from the dark ages". The academic articles were time well spent. They provided me with an invaluable repository from which I drew later, whenever I was asked to provide something for publication at short notice. These writings provided the genesis of publications in Ireland and laterally, in New Zealand. This was something I could never have imagined would emerge from the original documents and my purpose in writing them.

My first visit to the hospital for a check-up was a positive experience. The medical team was happy with my progress and talk of putting me on Rituximab over a period of two years was a timely boost. Two years seemed like a lifetime of forever to me then! As a family, we were thrilled at the prospect of a two-year strategy, even though we were acutely aware that there was uncharted territory ahead of us. Uncertainty would be my constant companion now more than ever before in my life. Remission was the goal that had evaded me to date. While it was encouraging to hear long-term options, the failure of two previous courses of chemotherapy left me under no illusions with regard to outcomes. I had to tread slowly and carefully; build on the positives as I reached each landmark. The next weekly visit went well and it was followed a week later with a major boost to morale when my platelets were up to ninety-three! While a hundred is as high as they go, I was on track, or so it seemed.

Each subsequent weekly visit for blood tests and to have the Hickman line flushed proved positive, despite the few remaining side effects. I told myself to get over them. I had to believe that they would pass. Things were looking good. I convinced myself that I was making progress on many fronts. Nevertheless, it was a time for cautious optimism, a time to continue doing what I was doing and hope for the best.

Brian and Ronan were delegated the duties for St. Valentine's Day. Brian was assigned the task of purchasing a piece of jewellery for Mary in a jeweller's shop in the city. He phoned me a few days beforehand to tell me that he couldn't find the shop. However, after due discourse, it transpired that he was standing in front of the shop with his back turned to it. Ronan managed the visit to the florist as well as getting a card befitting the occasion. I considered this good training for them until I was informed that they were seasoned campaigners in this domain.

While cupid was directing the customs and practices of St. Valentine's Day, I got news from the Cancer Centre that a CAT scan was scheduled for 8th March. This scan would show how effective the last course of chemotherapy had been. It was a strange and unnerving time in that I was conflicted. I wanted to have the scan and I dreaded having it. This would be it, all or nothing. Partial remission was like short-term commuting of my death sentence. Full remission would give me more time. That was about the size of it in my view. Others might interpret it otherwise. It was my life and it was now balancing on a knife-edge.

I played down the time to the CAT scan in turbo-positive mental conditioning mode. I focused on the affirmative as I built up my walking stamina, supported by my canine friend, Buddy. I worked on positive thinking and visualised myself walking away from cancer. Every time we walked past a litter bin, I told Buddy that we threw our negatives into it. Whenever I lay in bed with the window open, I visualised pushing the cancer out through the soles of my feet and into the atmosphere where the sun burned it into cinders.

Spring was in the air and breaking out all over the place - fresh flowers peeked out everywhere, buds burst open in the bushes and trees, birds sang and busily built their nests. Those spring days roused all of nature to a green and growing chorus. Spring breathed life back into the tired and barren ground after the wet and cold of winter. Everything was cleansed and renewed. Once again, the black-plumed minstrel more popularly known as the blackbird with its gold bill led the avian choir in their recitals and stayed on mission with his peers - announcing the arrival of daybreak. Life was good as the countryside gradually threw off the cloak of winter; farm animals both young and old took to the lush, new green pastures with relish. Spring lifted my spirits with its brighter evenings and hope's promise that the year ahead would bring happy days and warm sunshine to light the path of my recovery. Spring always gave me hope and inspired my dreams for the year ahead. 2006 was no exception. I had to have hope; the alternative was simply unthinkable. The words from Andy Dufresne's letter to Red in *The Shawshank Redemption* were of particular significance; "Hope is a good thing, maybe the best of things, and no good thing ever dies." Hope was about the only thing we had to sustain us.

CHAPTER TWELVE

The Murky Depths

"You're never beaten until you admit it."
- General George S. Patton Jr.

The lows came in both physical and emotional guises. The night sweats returned a few nights after I was released from hospital. Even though the medical team had advised me to expect them, they proved a stark and horrible reminder that the cancer was still active and continuing to make its unwelcome presence felt. It was sending me a clear message that it was not prepared to go away quietly. It would not capitulate easily. It had invaded and captured my body. It had taken up long-term uninvited and unwelcome occupancy. The war was far from over and the cancer had won every round of every fight so far. I had spent fifteen months on the back foot losing all the time, and while nobody likes to lose, I was a particularly bad loser all my life. I absolutely hated losing and here I was, losing the most important contest of my life.

It was not a time for self-pity or a faint heart. In rugby terms, I would have to make the hard yards. There were times when I am sure poor Buddy thought I was the nearest thing to a demented cuckoo clock as I ranted and raged against my destructive and evil enemy. I was angry with myself and hurled all sorts of expletives and every form of verbal abuse in my vocabulary at the cancer. It was my way of coping, and in some crazy manner, of convincing myself that maybe I could force an exorcism of the evil that had taken destructive control of my body. This rage kept me going at a time when my entire world was falling apart. I was in danger of having a Lusitania experience - torpedoed by cancer, sinking quickly and leaving Mary, Brian and Ronan the survivors of my voyage.

The night sweats were followed by bouts of the dreaded rigors. They were more violent than they had been previously. Whenever they struck, I had to go to the hospital where I was seen by a doctor immediately. Once the doctor was happy that it was only the rigors, I was allowed home again. The shaking and shivering caused me to moan in pain and roll about on the floor in an effort to get relief. Sometimes it reminded me of a scene from *The Exorcist* - in some perverse way I had been possessed by cancer and it created a hell of a racket that caused my body to go into heavy sweats and violent bouts of the shakes as the medication fought to expel it from my body. Cancer was an evil illness, like a sinful and malevolent spirit inside me. It fought and fought to retain and destroy me. I had to fight back. I had to believe that although the going was tough, I could be tougher. It was like hitting the proverbial wall in the last few miles of a marathon when the body wilts with tiredness and you have to take yourself aside for a private word - "We did not come this far to give up." The difference between fighting the cancer and hitting the wall in the marathon is that in the marathon, you have some level of control over the situation. Once you cross the finishing line, the intrinsic reward makes all the effort worthwhile. However, when you're fighting with cancer, you never know whether the finishing line is remission or death!

As Professor Gupta had warned, the psychological lows arrived after a few weeks once I came down from the emotional high of coming home from hospital and dealing with the challenges of survival in my new and unusual circumstances. The lows always found me sleepless at night, or when I was alone during the day while everyone was at work. It took Buddy's best counselling skills to rescue me from the emotional morass in which I found myself. I realised that I was in an unenviable position, trapped with only one desired outcome. The journey was challenging for both mind and spirit. The route was daunting and uncompromising. The spirit was willing although the poor mind and body bawled at me for mercy as I pushed myself to the limit and demanded more. Pain and sickness were temporary and I would get over whatever was thrown at me. Joe Quinlan's words *"You owe it to yourself and your family"* were my mantra and battle cry - in my case, the battle cry of the weary.

Ronan dropped in to see me while I was resting in bed one morning shortly after I came out of hospital. He asked how I was and how I felt regarding my prospects of recovery. There was no point in trying the euphemistic route with Ronan, so I told him honestly what the situation was, in that I was waiting for a PET scan that would tell how or if the January procedure had worked. He told me that he was not taking anything for granted and he was not going to have his hopes dashed again like they were when the first cycle of treatment failed, even with a ninety-five percent chance of success. He explained that he had been certain that I would get remission for a few years from that first cycle and once that failed, he was devastated and did not want to have his hopes built up only to be dashed once again. It was crushing to watch him as he shared his emotional journey with me from the time I was diagnosed to that moment. I felt a horrible guilt for the pain my sickness had inflicted on him. Life was tough enough for him navigating his way through his teenage years, finishing secondary school, embarking on college life and so many more of the challenges of growing up without having matters compounded by the fear of losing his father.

The situation looked hopeless. I couldn't tell him I would be okay, because at that stage we were playing a waiting game and living in hope. There would not be any respite for Ronan until I got remission. Until then, he had braced himself for the worst outcome. We had all done likewise in as much as we could. On the positive side, we must have done something right somewhere along the way because at least he felt he could come to me, speak openly and let me know what was weighing heavily on his mind. There was nothing I could do to allay his fears because they were well founded, and in truth, I could empathise fully with him. We talked and we talked. It did not change the scenario, but I did feel that I had some idea of what and how he was thinking. Now that he had divulged his thoughts to me, I decided that I would do everything I could to keep the channels of communication open between us. Hopeless, helpless and paralysing as the situation was, we would work together to muddle our way through it!

There was no instruction manual to deal with this situation. I had to navigate emotional territory strengthened more by faith than confidence that we would survive. What use was compassion and pity to a young mind tormented by the prospects of what cancer had in store for us as a family? We'd had our many differences and there were times we went head-to-head on issues, nevertheless, Ronan did not want me to die. It was obvious from our conversation that morning that while he was hoping for the best outcome and despite his best efforts to be optimistic, he feared the worst. He also told me that when he was a child, nothing really bothered him because he believed that whatever it was, I could fix it. He'd believed that I would overcome the cancer when I was first diagnosed, but his childhood belief in my invincibility was shattered when I relapsed.

Brian followed Mary's course of action with regard to my illness and he researched it in like manner. He assumed a patriarchal role and wrapped us in his care as he changed from a carefree young man to the protector of the pack. It was a sudden and merciless awakening for him. I watched him cope with the uncertainty that wreaked havoc with our lives. I couldn't tell him that everything would be all right. Both of us knew that I had a killer disease. Unlike me, he had researched the condition and was well informed while I lived on a need-to-know basis. Brian was the one taking responsibility, leading, caring. I hoped he would be more patient with me than I had been with him over the years, especially when we'd had differences of opinion. I should have listened more to him and been more understanding with him like he was with me right now. Our roles were reversed and I was learning so much from him. The big difference was that he was good at this and had none of my many shortcomings. He had an innate understanding and I learnt from him - the manner in which he read each situation and coped with it without fuss. Resilient as ever, he got on with life and did not complain. Now, years later, I realise that he was overburdened then and I was stupidly unaware. It was a very difficult time for him and I am indebted to those who gave him support at work and in his social group during those challenging times.

My mother had difficulty comprehending "why everything was taking so long". Although I had cancer, I felt that she thought my illness should be cured at this stage. It can't have been easy on her, and the fact that I was confined and unable to visit her did not help the frustration she felt. Even though she had strong belief in her religion and in prayer, there were times that she wavered in her faith and her patience weakened when it seemed to her that "nobody was listening to her prayers!" Whenever she was having a moment of protest, she could be quite entertaining and lifted the spirits of those around her when she gave vent to her dissatisfaction. Eventually, she must have had some indication that her prayers were getting some heed when Mary and I travelled to West Clare to visit her and take her out for lunch at the end of February. I think she was both relieved to see me and shocked by my physical appearance.

It was a little disconcerting for her when people did not recognise me in the restaurant where we had lunch, even though I was by now well used to the fact that the medication had greatly changed my physical appearance. However, it was never easy on the people I met, and it was clear from their reactions that it affected them deeply. I usually countered any uneasiness by playing the optimistic card with everyone I met; anything else would have been unthinkable. We usually exchanged pleasantries and I made a point of enquiring for all of their kin, young and old. At times I feared that I would make the mistake I made on one occasion when I was talking to somebody I hadn't met for some time. I asked how his mother was keeping, to which he replied that she had died a few years previously and that I had attended her funeral.

While I did my best to present an outwardly positive and optimistic face, I was not always in an upbeat mood because by this stage, I was an emotional wreck. In retrospect, it was inevitable because I'd encountered disappointment so often. However, I did my best not to burden people with my woes and court sympathy. I do admit that I wilted both mentally and physically while the weary old body ached as I shuffled about. In times of frustration, I would have to ask Buddy to cover his ears while I resorted to a full range of expletives to vent my frustration and anger when we were alone during the day and the situation seemed to be slipping out of my grasp. He always obliged and once I had blown off a head of steam and restored some semblance of emotional equilibrium, I would share with him my philosophies on life. He is an intelligent animal and always wagged his tail approvingly. I rewarded him with a treat for his palate and a walk. Once the siege lifted, I would convince myself that there were some positive signs emerging as the person who looked out at me from the mirror became a little more recognisable.

CHAPTER THIRTEEN

Land! Newfound Horizons

"The darkest hour is just before the dawn"

- Thomas Fuller (1650)

The waiting period for the CAT scan was beyond unnerving. I felt the hangman's rope was dangling from the gallows above my head and it would remain there until we got the results. The waiting would take forever. We had to meet the outcome head on.

The scan was a routine procedure, softened by a series of goodwill text messages. Then the waiting began. Clouds of doubt fogged my mind. Idle talk of nurturing positive thoughts irritated me in light of my experiences in the previous fifteen months. I had been at the wrong side of the statistics on two previous courses of chemotherapy; I had lived a reasonably healthy lifestyle and found myself with a killer disease. I had a wife and family of two boys, an ageing mother, a handful of relatives and a small circle of friends together with Buddy the dog, who in all probability would not have me long-term in their lives. I was like a fish just landed and gasping in its last moments of survival before suffocating. Cancer had been choking the life out of me and winning the war. What would the scan results reveal?

Two days later on Friday, 10th March after lunch, I got a telephone call from the Cancer Centre. It was not the result we were hoping for. While there was some improvement, preliminary results showed that there was still cancer in my body.

As far as I understood, it bought me some time but in light of my relapse experience over the previous summer, it looked like the angel of death had only postponed its visit. Mary, Brian and Ronan were equally disappointed - a cloud of doom enveloped us. Life and experience had taught us. My mother, together with my nephew Ciaran O'Neill and his wife, Fiona, were equally dejected. I had played my last ace and failed to get remission. Ronan made no secret of how cheated he felt at the prospect of losing me to cancer. Brian was deeply despondent. The carefree life they had known up until sixteen months previously was gone. Instead, they faced the prospect of losing their father to cancer.

I had an appointment with Professor Gupta three days later on Monday 13th March. He explained that although all the cancer had not been cleared, there was a great reduction in the tumour size subsequent to the recent high-dose chemotherapy. He would schedule a PET scan in the Mater Hospital in Dublin. This scan would determine the nature and extent of my condition and what the future might hold. The jury was retiring once more pending further evidence!

The next few days were emotional. I was relieved that the tumour was greatly reduced and disappointed that I hadn't gotten full remission. During the week, the hospital contacted me to complete the paperwork for the PET scan scheduled for the following Monday, 20th March. I was also given details on how to prepare for it. As the results would be definitive, I grew more anxious as the days passed and by the eve of the event, I was really on edge. I did the best I could to mask my anxieties from my family but the tension was palpable. Also, I had a terrible pain in my lower back which I had decided not to mention to anybody, probably because I was seriously concerned that it was quite similar to the one I'd had in August the previous year before my relapse. There would be time enough to unload my concerns if I really needed to. It was a classic example of the old saying - "It will be time enough to bid the devil good morrow when I meet him". I would wait and see what the scan revealed.

The week leading up to the PET scan in Dublin was difficult. I was in conflict with myself in that I wanted to have the scan in the hope of a favourable result while I also dreaded the prospect of an unfavourable outcome. My nieces, Anne and Fiona O'Neill, were welcome visitors on St. Patrick's Day, and helped to distract us from the anxiety that was building in advance of Monday's scan.

Mary drove me to Dublin on the day of the scan. The conversation was sporadic en route to the hospital. When we arrived, the procedure took place on time. The process took three hours from beginning to end. I had to remain still for the entire duration of the scan since motion would reduce the quality of the images. It began with an injection into a vein in my arm and after forty-five minutes, I had to drink a liquid tracer that travelled through my body and was absorbed by the organs and tissues being studied. Next, I was asked to lie down on a flat examination table that glided into the centre of the PET scanner; a doughnut-shaped machine. This machine detected and recorded the energy given off by the tracer substance and, with the aid of a computer, converted this energy into three-dimensional pictures. A physician then looked at cross-sectional images of the body organ from any angle in order to detect functional problems. The actual scan took about forty minutes, the last ten of which were the most uncomfortable. It was difficult to stay in position while trying to cope with an overwhelming urge to go to the toilet, the result of consuming so much liquid in preparation for the scan. Once the procedure had been completed, we set out on our journey home. And so began another session of wait and see while we counted down the days until the results of the scan were available to us. In the meantime, we continued to live with the uncertainty and fear that had haunted us for the previous sixteen months.

The phone rang four days later. The cancer liaison nurse from the Cancer Centre told me that the prognosis was very favourable, as were the PET scan results. I would have an appointment with Professor Gupta on Monday to discuss his plans for the future. The good times were back after a brief and painful absence. The siege was at last lifted; my one-way ticket to somewhere over the rainbow would be post dated for a greater period of time and it felt great. I felt like the phoenix rising from the ashes; reborn and renewed.

All of us were elated. There were tears of relief and joy. There would be no looking back. It was hard to believe that our luck had changed. Our relief was beyond description. Mary, Brian, Ronan and I went out for dinner that evening to celebrate. We had so much to celebrate after so many disappointments so we savoured our new fortune. Mary and I went to West Clare on Sunday for Mother's Day to spend it with my mother. We had so much to be thankful for.

I met Professor Gupta on Monday after spending the weekend savouring the good news. It was great to meet with him and hear his professional opinion on the results of the PET scan. He also filled me in on the option of going on a course of Rituximab, which is a drug aimed at keeping me in remission.

Rituximab is a monoclonal antibody that has been used on patients worldwide. It is used to treat certain types of non-Hodgkin's lymphoma by specifically targeting a marker (called CD20) on the B-cells in which most non-Hodgkin's lymphoma starts. It would be infused every twelve weeks when I attended for a check-up. The initial plan was to go on a course for two years. Two years sounded like an eternity as I had just been rescued from the jaws of death by Professor Gupta and his medical team. I decided to go with the Rituximab option. I felt that it gave me a greater chance of staying in remission. The first treatment was scheduled for Monday, 10th April. Professor Gupta and the medical team had done the oracle for me. Two years of treatment, I told myself. That would buy me time while medical science progressed, and with the good fortune that had just come my way, there was reason to be optimistic. I was now officially in remission. It was a time to seize the moment. Suddenly, the world was a wonderful place full of promise, opportunity and prospects once more. I grounded myself with the old Irish proverb; "Steady yourself and go carefully when your jug is full!" However, there was a moment tinged with sadness when I thought of the patients I met on the journey who had been less fortunate. Regrettably, they are no longer with us. Their families are left with empty chairs and empty places at the dining table.

"The rung of a ladder was never meant to rest upon, but only to hold a man's foot long enough to enable him to put the other somewhat higher." Thomas Henry Huxley; Life and Letters of Thomas Huxley.

I returned to the hospital for blood tests the day after my consultation with Professor Gupta. It was a pleasant experience to return to the team in the

Cancer Centre who had journeyed through the cancer experience with me and my family. I needed to be discreet with regard to my remission because the last thing any of the other patients at the centre needed was someone in triumphal or *"high-five"* mode while they dealt with their own situations. I could empathise with them. None of us wanted to be there yet we realised it was our only hope in the fight with the evil disease. The medical team was happy that I was in remission as each member had played a part in getting me over the bad days and on to the path that I would now travel.

The blood tests showed that my haemoglobin levels had dropped to 8.5 and so I would need a blood transfusion. That was a bit of a shock to the system after the euphoria of the previous week. It brought me abruptly back to the reality of living with cancer. Even though the fact that I was in remission was a major milestone, it was not the journey's end. Life was now an ongoing quest during which I would have to take whatever routes necessary. This was a reality check. I had the blood transfusion the next day at the Cancer Centre, which was an all-day event. Soon afterwards, I had the Hickman Line that was inserted in my chest before Christmas removed. It had become embedded in my flesh and took some work on the doctor's part to remove it. However, it was a major psychological event for me, not least because its removal symbolised an end to a very precarious period in my life. I focused on rebuilding myself by way of healthy eating and walking, but it was not a totally Spartan lifestyle - we indulged ourselves from time to time!

I had my first Rituximab treatment on Monday, 10th April. I had blood tests first, and while I was waiting for the results, I had a consultation with Professor

Gupta. We discussed the prospect of when I might return to work and after due consideration, we agreed that I would go back to work on Tuesday, 2nd May. It was an exciting and unnerving prospect. It signalled a host of positives. Medical opinion considered me well enough to return to work. I was out of the sick zone and fit to work again.

Once the blood test results came back from the laboratory, infusion of the Rituximab began into a vein in my arm. The drug had to be infused slowly and monitored closely to ensure that I did not have an adverse reaction. Everything went according to plan, and once the procedure was finished around three o'clock, I was allowed to go home. This was the first infusion into my arm since December when the Hickman Line was inserted. I considered this another positive on the journey. The only side effects I experienced from the Rituximab were nausea and a hangover feeling for a few days. It was a small price to pay - I was not complaining.

During a consultation, the medical team psychologist assured me that my mental attitude was a great asset in my journey from cancer to remission. To be honest, there were times when I wasn't quite sure what she thought of my coping mechanisms. In retrospect, I know I often hid my real feelings and fears by putting on a brave face while I was disintegrating emotionally and psychologically. I know that there were times when I was given credit for fighting and remaining positive when it was all a great pretence on my side. Maybe I did it out of vanity, maybe it was an effort to protect those near and dear to me. I am not sure, and it would be disingenuous of me to pretend otherwise. I think I just did what I did to survive, nothing more and nothing less. But there was more to come.

Three days later on Thursday, 13th April, I suffered a terrible pain in my back. I did not make an issue of it to my family but decided to get it checked out at the hospital the next day. On my way there, I felt very ill and had to pull the car over to the hard shoulder and rest a while before making the rest of the journey to the hospital. Thankfully, I felt much better as the day progressed and once I was checked out by the medical team and feeling well again, I was discharged. It was a reminder that while I was in remission, I was still and would remain under medical care. In a way, this was part of the aftermath of my battle with cancer. On a less dramatic note, I would remain a member of the cancer community. That was my reality.

The next task was to organise certificates of fitness and put arrangements in place to return to work with LDS. Returning to work was certainly going to be quite a change from the inactive life I had lived since Christmas. The evil gremlins threw a wild party as they planted all sorts of doubts and anxieties in my mind, taunting me in the dark of night. I was also very aware that even though I was away from work for just over four months, everything would have gained momentum in my absence and I would have to hit the ground running. Anything less and I would be found wanting, perish the thought! My pride and professional reputation were at stake. I braced myself and entered the fray on Tuesday, 2nd May at a team meeting in Athlone, its hinterland one of the last habitats of the corncrake.

*May 4th 2006 - Mary, Buddy & I on the week I returned to work,
14 weeks after coming home from hospital.*

It was both an exciting and an overwhelming experience. I harboured doubts about whether I would have the stamina to cope with travelling the length and breadth of the country and working in various centres. Delivering programmes to colleagues was a daunting task at the best of times, not to mention coping with broadside and blindside remarks from those attendees who did all in their power to derail, discredit and undermine. Dealing with the woodpeckers was an occupational hazard. I often thought it a pity that those with closed minds were not blessed with closed mouths.

Fortunately, the cynics were few and the vast majority of the people I met were consummate gentlemen and ladies. The seminars for teachers provided a major source of learning through the collective wisdom of the groups. They reminded me of the gatherings the native Americans held when they parleyed, or the deliberations of our ancestors here in Ireland at "óenachs" and fairs in bygone days. The experience with my colleagues from the teaching fraternity brought meaning to the dictum, "cynics criticise, experts analyse." It was an experience to witness the zeal with which those with a vocational commitment to teaching evaluated the evolution of education policy, philosophy and practice with enthusiasm and excitement borne from insight gleaned during their time at the cold face of the Irish primary education system. They brought the passion for learning and the spirit of the Bardic schools into the twenty-first century. There were also some great occasions at the end of the day's work when it became clear that the craft of storytelling was alive and well, as was the tradition of a good old sing-song.

CHAPTER FOURTEEN

Time and Tide Go On

"We are made to persist. That's how we find out who we are."

- Tobias Wolff, *'In Pharaoh's Army'*

I went to a senior rugby match in Dooradoyle between Garryowen and Shannon with Michael O'Brien on the Saturday following my return to work. Matches between these two proud rivals are usually great events and the banter on the sidelines between the rival fans is as keen as the competition on the field. This event proved no exception. Exchanges on the pitch were unyielding and manly in every regard, in keeping with the competition between these two great sides. No man on the field was safe, not even the unfortunate referee, whose pedigree and progeny were called into question by each and every wag present. Even his mother and sisters got dishonourable mention!

I met with Mark Fitzgerald, a former colleague from work and his friend David Wallace of Munster Rugby fame. We chatted for a short while and I wished David the best of luck in the forthcoming Heineken Cup Final before we went our separate ways. Two weeks later, David Wallace and the Munster rugby team won the Heineken Cup and were crowned European Club Rugby Champions. Limerick hosted unbridled celebrations. The win was borne out of two previous near misses, lots of disappointment and criticism despite their hard work, and the team's ruthless recovery from setbacks - the prize was well and truly theirs.

Munster's win lifted all our spirits and their capacity to rise above their disappointments was influential in kick-starting me to set targets for myself, one of which was to get back to doing a little jogging and get fit. So, on the 29th April, I shuffled four rounds of the running track at the University of Limerick Sports Arena. The pace did not threaten any land speed records or inflict scorch marks on the running surface. Anybody who might have seen me would have been forgiven for thinking, "If that fellow goes any slower, he will get a parking ticket". Neither pace nor performance concerned me on this occasion because in my own mind, I was having a triumphant return to the great outdoors. I savoured every moment of it. I was actually living out one of the dreams that sustained me while I was in hospital. I was thrilled with myself. The psychological and emotional boost this simple act afforded me was priceless.

The long lay-off from exercise combined with my medication and the medical procedures I had undergone had taken their toll on my physical condition. Although my body ached all over for almost a week after my efforts on the running track, the discomfort did not bother me because it was another great step forward on my road to recovery.

On Sunday, 2nd July, while I was on one of my newly-commenced regular visits to my mother, we were passing through Doonaha when we noticed a lot of activity at the football field. We soon discovered that the community was holding a family day. We met people from the parish that I hadn't seen for quite some time. There were smiles all around as people shook my hand and told me how pleased they were to see me in remission. It was great to be alive. I decided to round off the day with a swim in Haugh's Strand. The water never felt better, everything about the place was just perfect as I looked down from cloud nine. Eventually, the sun began to sink behind the horizon and I had my tea with my mother before I set out for home. I listened to *Days Like This* by Van Morrison several times on the road back to Limerick where I learned from my good friend Michael McMahon that his wife Anne had relapsed and was back on treatment. Cancer took Anne subsequently.

I tried to curb my enthusiasm and be patient as I gradually built up my stamina until 27th August when I ran the four-mile route that I had run on the 4th December, 2004, prior to noticing the lump in my neck that set the diagnostic wheels in motion. Although it was a non-event to the rest of the world outside of my family, it was a landmark event in my mind. Now I was moving in the right direction and that meant the world to me, selfish though it might sound. Maybe I was self-obsessed. I would prefer to think that I was driven by the will to recover and get out of the snare in which I'd been entangled for more than twenty-one months.

I had unfinished business with the West Clare Mini-Marathon and set my sights on getting fit to run it in the coming January. However, a combination of work schedules and sports injuries conspired to cause me to miss it. Having missed it once again, I resolved that time was of the essence and that I would be at the starting line in 2008. At that point, I doubt I would have passed the human equivalent of the NCT. Nevertheless my good friend and physiotherapist, Colum Flynn, had me in good running shape and despite outward signs of wear and tear, he had me ticking over nicely physically. The extensive coverage my participation received in the Clare Champion before the event was an added pressure to complete it. Accompanied by Brian, I took a place at the starting line in Carrigaholt more in trepidation than confidence. Mary and my mother Annie provided moral support. Mary's words, "Remember how far you have come from your sick bed and don't worry about how fast you can run!" made perfect sense to me by the time we had climbed Moyarta Hill. My legs were turning to jelly and my lungs were gasping for more of the clean sea air by the time we reached the top of the hill! However, it was not a time to be faint hearted so I bit the bullet and kept my sights on the finishing line.

It was an auspicious occasion as Brian and I ran side by side all the way to the finishing line in Kilkee, completing the 6.75 miles in fifty-seven minutes with a sweaty and emotional embrace. It was a wonderful feeling. I felt that I had cheated death to complete the run that cancer had denied me three years earlier. Brian and I went on to complete the run from Doonbeg to Kilkee the following year in 56 minutes. On that occasion, my godmother, Mrs. Mary Flanagan, was out to lend me moral support near Béal Átha church. Soon afterwards, when I began to slow down as we attacked the climb on Farrihy Hill a few miles north of Kilkee, Brian had to give me very direct vocal encouragement to ensure that I did not drop off the pace we had set for ourselves. The downhill run into Kilkee and getting over the finishing line brought closure to another event on the list. We rounded off the event with a swim in the Atlantic for good measure. Next on the list was the inaugural Monaleen Cancer Support 10K on Mothers' Day, 22nd March. It looked like every man, woman and child in the parish had turned out for it. There were runners, walkers, children in buggies and myself, shuffling. I crossed the finishing line in fifty minutes and nine seconds, a little annoyed not to break the fifty minutes mark.

Brian and I nearing the finish line in the West Clare Mini-Marathon - January 2008

After the Monaleen event, I took part in the Clare 250 Mile Cycle for Cancer Support at the end of May. Shortly before the event, I took a bad fall from the bike at a railway level crossing when my front wheel got caught in the railway tracks. I remember crashing to the ground and feeling the worse for wear as I got to my feet. Thankfully, I was wearing a cycling helmet - otherwise my injuries would have been much worse because the helmet was badly damaged in the fall. Once I composed myself, I mounted my trusty iron steed and continued homewards. After a few days, I felt the ill effects of the fall. My ribs were damaged and caused me serious discomfort whenever I moved, sneezed, laughed or coughed. I knew the pain from previous experiences with rib injuries. Once again I had to depend on the ever-obliging and reliable Colm Flynn to carry out running repairs. True to form, he had me back on the saddle quickly and ready to tackle the 250-mile challenge when I went to the starting line a few weeks later.

The Clare 250 Mile Cycle took us on a circuit from Ennis around East Clare on day one to villages and parts of the county that I had never seen until then. As we left Ennis on the first leg of our tour, we had torrential rain that made me wonder what would happen if it continued for the duration of the cycle. Not a pleasant thought, but before long, the gods smiled on us and the rain cleared as we entered Tubber, a place I had never been to before. The tea in Tubber was like a magic potion in the manner in which it revived me after the morning's drenching. From Tubber, we headed for Tulla, where we had our first test on the hills before heading north-eastwards through Bodyke and on to the beautiful lakeside towns and villages of Tuamgraney, Scarriff, Mountshannon and Whitegate, where we had lunch. Then we retraced some of our tyre tracks before swinging left for Ogonneloe and Killaloe, where talk and thoughts turned to the King of the Hills trial at Truagh. The climb at Truagh generated intense competition amongst the serious cyclists in the group, while it was a test of endurance for more of us. Getting to the summit was our sole objective, regardless of where we were positioned.

I was one of those bringing up the rear of the group and felt happy to survive it. I found that as we attacked the hill, I went into oxygen debt as my lungs ached while I pushed for the summit. My will wilted as my lungs paid the price of some of the side effects of my medication. I dismounted, and following a severe bout of coughing that cleared my lungs, I was able to breathe properly again. Once I composed myself, I phoned Mary and her words of advice and encouragement were the elixir I needed to get me astride my trusty iron steed once again and carry me on my way *"ar nós na sí gaoithe"* (like the fairy wind).

After the challenge of the climb at Truagh, it was almost a freewheel spin into Sixmilebridge, onto Newmarket-on-Fergus and into Ennis. From there, we pushed on into Lisseycasey, where we slept on the local hall floor in sleeping bags. Although the going was challenging at times, I was buoyed by the hospitality in every town and village where we were treated to refreshments and culinary delights to sustain us on our journey.

The second day was reminiscent of times gone by in Ireland; we got up and cycled to mass in Kilmihil. We ate again after mass before priming our trusty mounts and setting out on our journey westward, taking in Cooraclare, Kilrush and Kilkee before heading northwards on the coastal route through Doonbeg, Mullagh, Quilty, Miltown Malbay, into Lahinch and on to Ennistymon. The climb out of Ennistymon had everyone out of the saddle and several groans were audible as tiredness began to take its toll. Once out of Ennistymon, the pace increased significantly and at times, most of us were going flat out. It felt like the group was driven on by a sniff of home, sensing that we were nearing the home straight. It was like an image from a Christy Moore song as we rode like the fairy wind through the Burren, Lisdoonvarna and into Kilfenora.

By the time we hit Corofin, the sun was setting in the west and it was time to put on the lights and reflective gear. The final stages of the cycle from Corofin continued at a lively pace and the encouragement we received from people who came out in large numbers to cheer us on only added fuel to our push for home. Every man, woman and child from Ruan and its hinterland came out to cheer us onto the last leg of our journey. After Ruan, the street lights of the county capital were a welcome sight in the night sky ahead of us. Mary was waiting for me when we arrived at the finishing point in Ennis. Both of us were elated that I had conquered the challenge. It was quite a journey from the "circuit training" in the hospital corridor of January 2006.

While it was a daunting task for me, it proved to be a wonderful one in that I met some of the greatest people one might wish to meet. There were cyclists from all over Clare taking part, and every one of them had their own story to tell on how cancer had invaded, and in some instances taken, someone close to them. The peloton was led into each village and town by participants from the local community. Caroline Roche from Doonaha, Michael Shannon from Cross and I led it into Kilkee.

Once I had completed these fundraising events, I decided to absent myself from the cancer fundraising circuit. This decision was borne out of survivor's guilt on my part. I was afraid that it might appear to some that I was brash or triumphalist in my remission, especially through the eyes of families bereaved by cancer. I have failed to attend funerals of people who died of cancer because I had neither the heart nor the courage to do so when those who soldiered with me in the Cancer Centre were less fortunate than I. It is difficult to shake a bereaved person's hand and utter words of condolence while I stand there like the cat with nine lives because I had luck on my side. It is a fine line that continues to bother me.

Damned if I do go to funerals and damned if I don't. However, my door is open to those unfortunate enough to be diagnosed or bereaved. Everyone has a story to tell, some more painful than others.

Having survived the cancer era, Mary and I decided to pamper ourselves with a few holidays. The first one we took was a much-needed break in Sirmione on the banks of Lake Garda in Northern Italy in August 2006. It was a fabulous holiday and the hospitality accorded to us by the people running the hotel was wonderful in every respect. We took a few other trips too - we visited the US, Spain, Italy and New Zealand.

I worked with LDS until the end of August, 2009 and returned to the role of principal of Galvone N.S. on 1st September. It was time for me to move on from LDS. I had had enough of living out of a suitcase as a way of life, together with moving from venue to venue every few days, which had become a chore in itself. We worked in centres as far away as Gweedore in Donegal and Dunmanway in Co. Cork. Weekends were frequently spent preparing work. There were times when I had to work on Saturdays and sometimes I had to leave home on a Sunday to have things ready to roll on a Monday morning wherever I was scheduled to be. There was also a study trip in 2006 to Boston College, Massachusetts and Boston College, San Francisco, which turned out to be a ten-day busman's holiday.

The trip started on a sour note when the agent at passport clearance in Shannon had difficulty reconciling the facts that my passport stated I was a teacher while Boston College documentation identified me as a scholar. Having received clearance to travel at Shannon, little could I have imagined what lay in store for me on my arrival stateside! When I reached passport control, two armed officers in uniform told me to accompany them.

Despite my best efforts to convince myself that this was regular procedure, the signs were ominous. They escorted me to an elevator and instructed me, "Step inside. When you reach downstairs, you will enter a room where you will be interviewed!" I became extremely worried as this scenario played out. I began to think, "What if somebody had acquired the social security card I had when I worked in New York in the seventies and fallen foul of the law?" and, "Did I survive cancer to get locked up in the US?" This was real-life TV drama unfolding and I was at the centre of it!

When I entered the room downstairs, it was clear that I was not entering a hospitality suite. The walls were bare and the furniture bore all the hallmarks of an interrogation cell from a film. I was invited to state the reasons for my trip to the US, which I did succinctly, explaining that I was a guest of Boston College on an education trip. At that point, my interviewer grabbed a phone and made his annoyance at the manner in which I had been brought to his attention quite clear to whomever he was speaking. When he put down the phone, he apologised to me for how I had been treated, wished me a good trip to the US and assured me that he would be taking issue with those responsible for my upset and embarrassment. I told my interviewer that I was considering taking the next flight out of the US home to Ireland with a firm resolution never to return. This seemed to unsettle him and it became more obvious to me that I had been the victim of an overzealous agent. I was in no humour for this "kiss and make up" carry-on and took my leave without hesitation. When I emerged from my underground adventures, the rest of the study group were quite relieved as I rejoined them on the onward journey to our destination.

The people on the study trip with me formed a pleasant group from both sides of the Irish political divide, which proved a most enriching experience for me. Things were progressing seamlessly until I began to feel unwell after a few days on the trip. While the alarm bells sounded inside my head, I decided not to divulge to the others that I was not feeling too well. I resolved that there was nothing I could do about it until I got home, so I bit the bullet and got on with the work in hand. When I arrived home, I had a colonoscopy, and to my great relief, it was negative. The eventual conclusion was that the discomfort I suffered in the US was more than likely due to the high level of preservatives in the food I ate there.

On a lighter note, back in good old Ireland, I remember one Sunday evening when a few of us gathered in a hostelry in a certain part of Ireland. Some locals had observed our arrival from their vantage point in the bar as we checked in at reception. While we were being attended to, some of the patrons of the house took it upon themselves as good keepers of the community to enquire as to the nature of our business in the area. I advised them that we were on government business and that we would be in the parish for as long as it took to ensure that the affairs of the people were in order and that part of our remit was to be on the look-out for unlicensed bulls. Later in the evening, the proprietor of the venue informed us that news of our arrival had spread like wildfire and that bulls of every description in the parish were housed for the duration of our stay, regardless of the mating needs of the cows. I hoped that the contagion would not spread to cause undue abstinence to rams, drakes, ganders, cockerels and the like!

While I was putting the finishing touches to my work with LDS, I was scheduled for a CAT scan on 26th June, 2009. Although I had attended for all of my twelve weekly check-ups, and the infusions of Rituximab were going according to plan, a scan was never something I looked forward to. I kept telling myself that I felt good and hoped for a favourable outcome. Nevertheless, the day I had the scan, the rituals were all too familiar to me to offer any comfort. Drink the liquid, sit and wait to be called with my head buried in any reading materials available. Suddenly, the name of a well-known Limerick person was called and immediately, all heads suddenly turned to see if we were in the company of this person. Then a lady of the same name stood up, looked around at us, smiled and said, "It happens all the time!" before she left the waiting room for her appointment.

My turn came in due course, and once the procedure was done, it was a case of waiting a few days for the results. Although we had every reason to be optimistic, our greatest expectations were surpassed when the results showed that everything was clear, that all the areas where the cancer had originally been were now normal. This was another major step forward in the right direction for me. We savoured the moment. It was as if another piece of the recovery jigsaw puzzle had just fitted seamlessly into place. It was dreams of days like this that made life worth living and fighting for, even when we could see no hope.

When I returned to school in September 2009, it took ten minutes to get there, a welcome change from the travelling of the previous few years. Once back at school, it was like I had never left, despite the fact that some new people had joined the staff and others had retired. Thankfully, most of the personnel I was used to liaising with before I went on secondment to LDS were still working in the same sections within the Department of Education and Skills. However, one day when I phoned a particular person there and identified myself, the person taking my call said, "Oh! Kevin it is great to hear from you!" before gasping, "I heard that you got very sick and died!" I laughed, assuring her that I was very much alive and that rumours of my demise must have been somewhat exaggerated.

The school year began on a very upbeat note with a presentation to our own Limerick, Munster and Lions rugby hero, Keith Earls, when he launched the school's fourth Green Flag for environmental awareness. We held a reception for our past pupil and prize-fighter, Willie Big Bang Casey, who went on to become European Bantamweight Champion later in the year. His message for the children was, "Get a good education and follow your dreams." We marked the occasion of the visit of our sporting heroes with the customary unveiling of plaques in their honour on the wall of the reception area of the school, where they joined well known figures from sport and politics who had already visited the school, such as former President Mary McAleese, former Minister for Education and Science, Mr. Micheál Martin, former World Heavyweight Boxing Champion, George Foreman and rugby legends Keith Wood, Peter Clohessy, Alan Quinlan, Tom Tierney and David Wallace.

The school also welcomed the introduction of violin classes for all its pupils. This initiative culminated in the foundation of a youth orchestra over the course of the school year. In spring, we introduced the Learning for the Smart Economy Information Technology Initiative. Local woman, Mrs. Kinsella, the 2009 Munster Carer of the Year, did us the honour of launching the programme, which provided each child in fourth class with a netbook (laptop). The initiative was the first of its kind in the school and introduced the pupils to IT as an everyday part of their learning. While all of this was going on around me, I decided to retire at the end of the school year. I announced my intention at the end of February to allow the Board of Management plenty of time to appoint my successor and ensure a seamless transition.

When the school year drew to a close, we said our farewells and went on summer holidays. I attended to the usual summer works in the school over the holiday period and had the school in readiness, as was my duty, when I handed over the keys to my successor on 31st August, 2010. Thus my career in teaching came to a close. Four years with LDS and thirty-one years in Galvone/Southill in the Southside of Limerick City. The people from the area were good to me in the time I spent with them. I hoped that somewhere, somehow I might have succeeded in doing a deed of kindness that helped somebody along the way in their journey through life. However, time and tide waits for nobody. I had taken the final bell mindful of the words of William Shakespeare: "Things won are done; joy's soul lies in the doing." With achievements and shortcomings of the past docked in the harbour of the heart, once again it was time for change in my life, come what may.

The time had come to move on and leave the Southside of Limerick City, where I had watched the rise and meltdown of Southill since 1975. When I began my teaching career, Southill was an inner-city community in Limerick City South made up of 1,160 houses built by Limerick Corporation between 1966 and 1972 to meet the housing shortage of the time. A large number of the people there worked in local factories in Limerick and Shannon, as well as in the defence forces. Life only moves in one direction and that's forward. Many of the pupils we taught over the years and their parents saw education as the currency of the future and used it to shape their destiny, which in turn gave them social and economic mobility outwards from the area. Consequently, Southill lost most of its community leaders and it has followed a downward social and economic spiral. Unfortunately, Southill has become a place of few positive moving parts either socially or economically. The social dynamic that is overflowing with negative excesses has become an uninviting environment for those of fragile body or will. It is a place where the human and physical landscape bears many of the social scorch marks of an uncoupled community. Consequently, it has become an area that is spiritually fallow and a place less travelled.

On reflection, the vast majority of people I met in the teaching profession were great people. These teachers enjoyed what they did daily, and in the process, gained personal satisfaction through improving the lives of those with whom they engaged in the formal education system. Such positive experiences have a profound effect on a learning environment where pupils, teachers, ancillary staff and parents are constantly exploring ways of improving outcomes for lifelong learning and citizenship in the school community. It was a privilege to be part of such a professional experience. I knew that I was leaving the school in good hands. It had an outstanding Chairman of the Board of Management in Very Rev. Fr. Pat O'Sullivan P.P. whom I found to be an absolute gentleman.

It was a humbling experience to work with such talented people and a daunting one to be their leader. There were still some who suffered from "doughnut syndrome". That group was invariably overworked, self-congratulatory, carrying the school on their backs since they entered the profession and they were unappreciated to boot. They were the people who claimed that the job was impossible. There were times when the wisdom of Walter Gropius (1888-1969), "The human mind is like an umbrella - it functions best when open." made perfect sense to me, or perhaps the Irish proverb, "Ní dhéanfadh an saol capall rás d'asal" - all the world would not make a racehorse from an ass.

However, I knew very well when I took on the job of principal in the school that I would have to make difficult decisions. There were always going to be times when I would need to say things to people that they *needed* rather than *wanted* to hear. It's all part of the job. You have to crack a few eggs if you want to make an omelette. Conscious that communication is a two-way street, I welcomed constructive criticism and took it on board for my own learning and for the good of all concerned. I would like to think that I always admitted it when I got something wrong, and apologised without reservation whenever such an occasion arose. I aspired to walk the walk as opposed to simply talking the talk.

I did not enter retirement with a list of things I wanted to do in my life. Rather, I decided to let life happen, and so it did. I neither thought nor planned, which proved both wise and rewarding because whenever something came my way, I had the luxury of letting it pass or embracing it. I found my way to the keyboard of the computer from time to time and wrote this account of my journey with cancer as a testament to my family and the good people who cared for me in a most difficult and traumatic period in my life. I had time to hone my culinary skills, and I had the opportunity to support young people who were job-hunting and preparing for interviews. I was able to mentor some third-level students, and I had the rewarding experience of being nominated research supervisor for Joe Lyons in his M.A. in Educational Management in Waterford Institute of Technology. Added to all this, I edited the Clare & Limerick Education Research Conference (2011) Journals and facilitated the publication of one of those research papers in New Zealand. I also edited the 2012 and 2013 Wexford Education Centre's Education Research Conference Journals. It was through the publishing of these journals that I came to meet Conor Holmes from Outside the Box Learning Resources (www.otb.ie) – the publisher of this book. I am now looking forward to working with Tipperary Education Centre in organising an Education Research Conference for Gaelscoileanna in

2014, which will be done through the medium of Irish, as will the subsequent research journal.

I had articles of my own published in journals in both Ireland and New Zealand, and was honoured with the privilege of being invited to speak at an education conference in New Zealand. Later in the year, I had an invitation as a Boston College Alumni to have coffee with the American ambassador, Mr. D. Rooney in Dromoland Castle on Friday, 9th December. Unfortunately, I had to decline the invitation because I had an appointment for a check-up and my 19th session of Rituximab in the hospital. My health had to take priority over any other engagements. There will be time enough for coffee.

2012 was a busy year with the Clare & Limerick Education Research Conference proving an outstanding success with eighteen Irish researchers presenting papers, together with many researchers of global renown. Subsequently, I was given the opportunity to edit the Wexford Education Centre Colloquium for Newly Appointed Principals Research Journal. The gods are smiling favourably in my direction because I have been invited to edit both journals again in 2013.

Later in spring, I joined the team of Contract Supervisors for Teaching Practice. After I finished my induction and training, I was given the opportunity to supervise and work with groups of student teachers on their undergraduate teaching practice placements in Galway City, Clonmel, in Co. Tipperary and in Cork. While I was in Clonmel, I had the good fortune to meet up with Paul Brett, who appointed me to St. Kieran's C.B.S. when I started teaching in 1975. A true gentleman and a born leader, Paul is the type of person that everybody respects. He was cool and calm whatever the situation and blessed with a great sense of humour. I was delighted to tell him once again how much we missed him when he moved from the school to his native town. Limerick's loss was certainly Clonmel's gain.

Working with the student teachers was enriching and challenging. The high standards that the vast majority of them set for themselves are nothing short of phenomenal. I found the grading of the teachers on teaching practice most challenging, mindful that it was a practical examination. Whatever grades I awarded them would have a bearing on their final results at graduation as well as in the competition for jobs. Consequently, I laboured long hours and endured sleepless nights before coming to some of those decisions. On a more uplifting note, I was thrilled with the teaching calibre of those student teachers. There was also great fulfilment in knowing that primary education would be in the hands of very professional, competent, committed and highly motivated teachers for generations to come.

With luck on my side, I will manage to stay in remission and everything else will be an additional benefit. Nobody knows. Of one thing I am certain - I will pack as much as I can into every second of every minute of every hour's reprieve I get. I borrow this philosophy from the late, great Noel Carroll, when asked if running would give one a longer life, he answered, "Running might not add more years to one's life but it gives more life to one's years."

CHAPTER FIFTEEN

My Present Simple

"Learn from yesterday, live for today, hope for tomorrow. The important thing is not to stop questioning."

- Albert Einstein

Ronan spent the summer of 2007 working in Toronto and 2009 in Chicago. He graduated in August 2009 from the University of Limerick. His graduation was a major landmark in that I had relapsed at the time of Brian's graduation in 2005, and Ronan had noted that he wanted me around for his graduation in 2009. My promise to him that I would do my best to be there was made solely in hope. He took a year out and set off alone on his travels at the end of January 2010. His adventure took him to Thailand, where he had to negotiate his way through the riots of 2010 to get out of the country, and on to his next destination, Cambodia. From there, he travelled on to Malaysia, Vietnam, Laos, Myanmar, Australia, New Zealand, Fiji, Hawaii and on to Vancouver in Canada before returning home to start his training contract in Limerick. While it was a great experience for him, we did breathe a sigh of relief when he came through the arrivals gate in Shannon Airport. The travel bug remains with him. It took him to China last year and more recently, inter-railing across Europe in June 2012. During this stint, he was interviewed by Croatian Television in Zagreb during the Ireland - Croatia game in the European Championship. I don't think he will ever have to worry about getting a job as a soccer pundit, since he predicted a one-all draw before Ireland went on to lose the game by three goals to one.

Brian and Ronan at Brian's
Graduation – September, 2005

Ronan and I at Ronan's
Graduation - August, 2009

I noticed that it took Ronan until recent times to speak openly about how my illness affected him, and the manner in which he was frightened and angered at the thought of cancer killing me. These days, he frequently remarks that it is great to still have me around. I assure him that it is great to be around.

Brian finished his training contract in April 2009, and inspired by the spirit of youth, both he and his partner, Méabh O'Dwyer, moved to Wellington, New Zealand to experience life in the Antipodes and the Rugby World Cup.

Although we knew that this was something they needed and wanted to do, we were sad to see them depart and at the same time, envious of their adventures while they travelled around New Zealand supporting the Irish Rugby Team in the World Cup in September and October 2011.

They made two trips home after they left in 2009, and Mary and I travelled over to see them in April 2011. It was a great trip and it was wonderful to see Brian and Méabh in their adopted land. The only downside of the trip to New Zealand came at the end when we had to say goodbye and leave them behind us at the airport when we were returning home. There was a terrible sense of walking away from them. The parting hurt again. Parting was nothing like Shakespeare's "Parting is such a sweet sorrow" in Romeo and Juliet. Indeed it was not; to Mary and me, it was the direct opposite. We were overwhelmed with a sadness that pierced our hearts and caused choking lumps in our throats.

My mother is no longer with us. She suffered a stroke on the 10th October, 2008, and passed away sixty-nine days later on 18th December. It was sad to watch her lose her independence and eventually succumb to illness. Unfortunately, I was not with her when she passed away. I had just arrived in Cavan town when I was contacted by the hospital to let me know that she was getting very weak. While I was setting out on the journey to be with her, I got another phonecall to tell me that she had passed away peacefully. In a way, she went as she would have wanted to go; quietly and without any fuss. I was sorry not to have been with her as she took her final leave. However, I had a chest of memories to treasure and they would sustain me, like sitting overlooking the

Pollock Holes at the West End in Kilkee, gazing across the bay at George's Head as she reminisced of days gone by, or we discussed and solved the problems of the world. "Bíonn súil le muir ach ní bhíonn súil le h-uaigh". There's hope from the ocean but none from the grave.

Ronan wrote the following tribute to my mother and delivered it at the close of her funeral mass before we took her to her final resting place beside my late father in Moyarta Cemetery:

In Memory of My Grandmother

Fear not that, which you have yet to behold.
The darkness is merely the threshold
To the Elysian Fields, where he waits
For you. His embrace,
Relinquishing twenty-one years

Our souls shall meet in the lapses of time,
My hand in yours and yours in mine.
We will meander down the canal
Amongst the swans and the geese.
We will linger in the golden vale,
While the lambs bleat,
And the collies chase their tails.
As the dolmens weep, we'll hear their call,
Round Moher's face and our native soil.

The karst Burren shall shelter our tears,

To leave us rest in Boyne's timeless solstice.

Now rest your head, your service is done,

To your kin, countrymen and those far flung.

Lives have been touched by your delicate whispers.

In our ears they shall always linger.

- *Ronan Haugh (18/12/08) ©*

Nowadays, Mary and I share the empty nest with our golden retriever, Buddy, since Brian and Ronan have moved out. Prior to my illness, Mary had taken up art lessons and painted some fabulous still life and beautiful works in inks and oils. I believe that she is in denial with regard to her talent as an artist. Her life was pitched upside-down and she never wilted. Someday soon I hope she will take out the paints and easel, and her unfinished painting of Labasheeda will at last get its long-awaited final touches.

I am in remission since the 24th March 2006. The seven years have been a roller-coaster ride with the usual ups and downs that life throws. The Celtic Tiger has met his maker, the conniving antics of our politicians, bankers and developers have been revealed. As a nation, we are battered and exhausted as we suffer the aftermath of clerical abuse and bid farewell to our finest as they put down roots on foreign shores. We all pay the price.

The Irish are a resilient people and we will survive this recession. We will, in the words of President Michael D. Higgins, "… transform the arid present into a fertile future." I believe that the indomitable spirit of the great people of Ireland at home and abroad will bring us through these challenging times. It will take considerable resources and effort on all our parts, but we will emerge a stronger people. We have to believe that most of the challenges in life are not impossible; sometimes we just have to try harder to achieve them.

It would be remiss of me to conclude without once again acknowledging the professional judgement of Dr. M. Shinkwin. His diagnosis set the whole journey in motion and his support every step of the way was invaluable. I must also acknowledge the professionalism, care and attention to detail of Professor Gupta and his team on our journey together from diagnosis in December 2004 to date. My gratitude to my sister Josephine O'Neill who offered to donate if required. My thanks too to blood donors, because without their gift of blood, I would not have survived. There was also my physical rehabilitation, for which I will be forever indebted to Colm Flynn and Anthony Geoghegan for their unfailing support. Anthony's strength and conditioning boards from his MRIP programme were particularly helpful. I recommend them to people of all ages for muscle recovery and injury prevention.

I had my nineteenth treatment of Rituximab on the 9th December, 2011, during which I met Clare hurling legend, Ger Loughnane. It was our first time meeting, and although we had mutual interests in education and sport, our common enemy dominated our conversation. He told me his story and then I told him mine. We shared our experiences with cancer and the strategies we employed in our respective fights for survival against this evil parasitic disease. Sharing our journeys is all part of the lifestyle for some of us who live in the cancer community. It provides us with solace and it gave me the will and energy to fight on. The intensity of the fight to stay alive is all-consuming; there is no place for complacency. Cancer never sleeps.

There were times when I felt that initial first-time conversations on meeting a fellow patient in the Cancer Centre day ward were reminiscent of the ballroom era in 1960s Ireland. The usual ice-breakers went something like: "How are you today?" followed by, "Is this your first time here?" and, "Do you come here often?" Predictably, these openers were followed by, "Where are you from?" and, "How did you get here?" Not to mention, "Do you come by yourself?", or "Did somebody drop you here?" and the ever-important, "How are you getting home afterwards?" Conversation generally progressed to where one worked or lived, and this in turn might fuel conversation around mutual acquaintances, past and present. The nature of one's ailment and the course or courses of chemotherapy taken were central topics of conversation. Great comfort was drawn from every positive outcome shared. A negative outcome or an unfavourable prognosis was neither disclosed nor pursued. It was our way of coping and dealing with our respective situations. We gave each other whatever we had to give.

I had my twentieth and final maintenance treatment of Rituximab on Friday, 2nd March 2012, after which I had an appointment with Professor Gupta on the 2nd of April. He told me that he was very pleased with the condition of my health and suggested that he would see me for a check-up every six months over the next few years, after which he hoped annual check-ups would suffice. This was exactly what all of us had worked for. We left the hospital elated after the consultation. We were finally at the opposite end of the emotional continuum to when I was diagnosed in December 2004. It was a wonderful feeling and we could hardly wait to share the news with those who had journeyed with us over the previous seven and a quarter years.

To add to the great news about my health, Brian and Méabh decided that they would come home to Ireland to live in July 2012. We were still basking in our run of good news when the phone rang shortly before 6 a.m. a few mornings later. My first reaction was, "Oh my God! Who could be calling at this hour unless there is something wrong?" It was Brian calling from New Zealand with the lovely news that he and Méabh had just got engaged. What a way for them to remember ANZAC Day! Life could hardly get any better and no-one complained as all the pieces of the jigsaw fell neatly into place. Christmas 2012 was such a perfect day, spent together. Happy days. It was a seismic change in fortune.

The larcenous nature of cancer, its habit of breaking in on us when we are least prepared and stealing the irreplaceable causes me to reflect on how fortunate I have been to get remission. My thoughts often travel to those I met regularly and befriended in the Cancer Centre with their families during the course of our treatment. There were also neighbours from West Clare namely, Maureen Haier, Martin Reidy, and Teresa Hogan, all of whom I met regularly when we attended for treatment at the Cancer Centre. There were others who were less fortunate than I, like my great friend John Casey from Sneem, Co. Kerry, who passed away in February, 1998, and one of nature's gentlemen, Bernard O'Shea from Caherciveen, Co. Kerry, who passed away in March 2011, together with many more, all taken by cancer.

My neighbours from Monaleen, Georgie Fitzpatrick and Geraldine O'Doherty passed away, victims of cancer, in spring 2009. Geraldine and Georgie were leading figures in the local Wren on St. Stephen's Day each year. We have fond memories of Geraldine taking me for a waltz around the road in front of our house on the previous St. Stephen's day when she called with the Wren to celebrate my return to good health. Georgie passed away on 6th February, just four weeks after he visited me and spent the night in a positive frame of mind. His last words before we parted were, "Do you know what Kevin? I am in such good form I could tog out and play a game of football for Kilkee and another game for Clare immediately afterwards!" He was determined that he would get remission from his next course of treatment and that we would swim in the Pollack Holes in Kilkee come Whit weekend (2009), after which he would return to school before the summer holidays. Sadly for George and his family, that dream would never come true.

Ronan's friend Kevan Malone died in an accident in Cork on the day of Georgie's funeral on 9th February. Kevan had attended Ronan's 21st birthday party just a few nights before the freak accident happened in Cork. We learned later that the two of them had made preliminary plans to spend the coming summer in Chicago.

Ronan wrote the following farewell to Kevan:

Farewell My Friend

The blue sky melted into a dense grey.

The zephyr rose to an almighty gale.

The first drop rested upon my forehead,

As I reached out to take your hand.

The emptiness resonated through me,

As I wondered where you could be.

The torrential rain bombarded all around,

Interrupted by the deafening sound,

Of Thor's colossal hammer thundering down.

It was pathetic fallacy at its finest,

But for it I had not wished.

I call your name and I'm greeted by silence.

Just open your lips and draw one more breath.

The time is nigh, that our paths must part,

Mine leads north, and yours leads south.

Someday our paths will cross again.

Until then goodbye friend.

- Ronan Haugh (09/02/2009) ©

On the night Kevan died, I had just reached Newbridge where I was scheduled to work with LDS for two consecutive days when Ronan contacted me to tell me the dreadful news. It took some time for the message to sink in. Then I decided that I would travel to Athlone to meet Ronan with a view to supporting him in his shock and grief. While my intentions were good, I will never forgive myself being an abysmal failure to Ronan on this occasion. Every time I spoke, only the wrong words came out.

Christmas 2011 in Monaleen was another time of mixed emotions. While children found it hard to sleep at the thought of Santa Claus' visit and what he might bring, cancer took another of our beloved neighbours, Patricia Flynn. None of us can imagine the heartbreak and loss felt by her husband, Jerry, and her family, Sinead, Seán and Aoife.

The sadness and loss wreaked by cancer continued. On 4th April, 2013, it struck closer to home taking Nora Garvey, wife of my brother-in-law, Donal Garvey. While Donal, Darragh, Colm and Roisín were dealing with their loss and preparing to lay Nora to rest, news arrived that Nora's younger sister, Vourneen Heffernan, had also passed on from this life about eighteen hours later on 5th April. Both Nora and Vourneen had battled with cancer for some time. It was a cruel blow to Vourneen's husband Pat, and two sons Ultan and Luke, whose fourteenth birthday was the same day that his mother was taken from him and his family.

Shortly afterwards, the inspirational sixteen-year-old Donal Walsh from Blennerville, Co. Kerry, was taken by cancer on 12th May, 2013, shortly after he made an impassioned plea to people contemplating suicide not to opt for a permanent, long-term solution to a short-term problem. The loss of so many people to cancer stirs a sadness that will ebb and flow for those of us outside the immediate family, but none can imagine the sense of loss and heartbreak felt by families who have lost loved ones to cancer. It is at times of unbridled grief like these that one wonders if the angels of mercy have deserted us.

I hope that someday soon, medical science will provide those of us in long-term remission with an even longer-term, doubt-free one. But what would you call it? Some of us in the parish of Monaleen and beyond have created our own "firewall" for dealing with cancer - we meet from time to time for tea and talk. Conversation can vary from the sublime to the ridiculous! There are times when we throw caution to the wind, abandon the healthy option at breakfast time and go out for a good old full Irish fry-up. Because that's what we need to do sometimes.

I was never a great pilgrim. Nevertheless, in June 2011 I decided to visit the shrines of Padre Pio in San Giovanni Rotondo and St. Matthew in southeast Italy in a pilgrimage of thanksgiving. Brian and Ronan were very entertained at the prospect of me travelling on my own because Mary always plans every detail of our holidays, so much so that on one occasion, I had to ask her at the airport where we were going. Consequently, they suggested that she should tie a label around my neck as I would inevitably get lost without her.

I travelled to the village of San Giovanni Rotondo, in the southeast of Italy, where Padre Pio spent most of his life and where his tomb can be found today. The modern town is dominated by the Capuchin Friary where the saint lived and died, and by the New Basilica, dedicated to St. Pio of Pietrelcina, built after his canonisation in 2002. Having paid homage and given thanks to Padre Pio for favours granted, I decided that I should do likewise with St. Matthew for his part in my recovery, and set out to visit St. Matthew's Monastery in the nearby town of San Marco in Lamis.

I enquired at hotel reception as to where I might find St. Matthew's Monastery, to be told that it was just outside the town, well within walking distance. Confident, with my map and Italian phrase book in hand, I set out on foot. After more than an hour walking and San Giovanni Rotondo lost behind me, I decided to ask a few people working in a field by the roadside how much further down the road my destination was. They assured me that I was at least heading in the right direction, but that it was about ten or twelve kilometres ahead. Deflated at the prospect of walking so much further and back again, and growing in confidence with my Italian communication skills, I decided to hitch a lift. Luck was on my side and I got a lift from the second car to come my way. However, due to a communication failure, the driver did not understand me when I asked to be dropped off at the monastery. He brought me all the way into the next town where it took me some time to find a bus that would take me out to the monastery.

Eventually, I reached my destination and attended to my business there. On completing my pilgrimage, I walked the few hundred metres to the bus stop where I boarded a bus back to San Giovanni Rotondo. To be doubly sure I was on the right bus, I checked with the driver who reassured me, pointing to the sign. However, he did not tell me that the bus, though it was bound for San Giovanni Rotondo, was taking a circuitous route via Foggia, which was an hour's journey, and that there would be a delay there for another hour before it set out for my destination. So what should have been a fifteen-minute direct journey took me three hours. In the end, I did make it home safely without taking any other scenic routes and my family derived great entertainment out of my experience, which of course proved their assertion that I was destined to get lost travelling on my own.

At this stage I am happy to be alive. That is not to say that I take everything with a smile. I am still a cranky git and my fuse is shorter than ever, maybe even worse! Sometimes I wonder if the illness has taken its toll physically on me in a number of ways. I do not have the energy levels I had previously. Getting out of bed in the morning was always one of my weak points and so maybe it is unfair or even inaccurate of me to blame the chemotherapy for my tardiness in the mornings.

Ever since I began the first course of chemotherapy, I have noticed that I need a lot more sleep than I required prior to it. If I fail to get enough sleep, I suffer the consequences. When I returned to work after the high-dose chemotherapy, I realised that I needed to allow more time in the morning to get myself up and ready for the day. It took me an hour and a half to get up, wash, get dressed and eat breakfast before setting out to work. Consequently, I had to get started at 6.30 a.m. or earlier, depending on the schedule for the day. I never lost much time eating breakfast, as my family joked that I ate it so fast that they sometimes suspected that I inhaled it.

Now the effort of fumbling out of bed to meet the day still seems to take an eternity. Every limb and muscle in my body groans in pain while I bring myself to a standing position and shuffle to the shower. Once I turn on the shower, it's like defrosting the car on a frosty morning as each muscle and joint creeps into life. Once the body has kicked in, I attend to the coughing and spluttering rituals caused by the permanent chest infection that is a side effect of the medication. Strangely enough, while I and my family have become accustomed to this as part of my morning routine, our poor dog Buddy still gets distressed and lends yelps of support as he comes to check that I am okay. Those who know me will testify that the language out of me every morning as I hurl verbal abuse at the source of the coughing is not the vocabulary one might use in public.

Man and dog relationships are well chronicled. However, mine with Buddy reached an unprecedented level when both of us were on courses of antibiotics. He was on two tablets twice daily while I was on one tablet twice daily, except when I managed to confuse his dosage with mine by putting both of us on two tablets twice daily. Fortunately, it was only the dosage I confused. What would have happened if I had confused our medication, I wonder? Perhaps it would have caused me to bark irrationally at the postman and chase cats with dogged enthusiasm – perish the thought!

My morning routine is a small price to pay. In fact, I get great satisfaction in getting that part of the day behind me and moving on. I am grateful to be back on my feet and able to work again. I am grateful to be alive and conscious that remission from cancer is a privilege denied to many. I never cease to be inspired and take energy to drive on from the positive vibes I receive from my family and others as I set out every morning to give my best efforts to whatever challenges or opportunities the day has to offer.

While I do my best not to be superstitious, it is hard not to notice that the number 13 has appeared ten times so far in my journey with cancer. There were thirteen days from my consultation with Dr. M. Shinkwin on 8th December, 2004 and the 21st December, when the surgeon who took the biopsy for analysis told me that I had cancer. I had the stem-cell transplant on the thirteenth month of my battle with cancer. Added to this series of coincidences, I ran thirteen marathons, six of them in under three hours and the others took me between 3 hours 18 minutes and 3 hours 38 minutes. However, I ran marathon number thirteen in 1994, the Boston City Marathon, and it took me 4 hours and 40 minutes, which was more than an hour slower than any of my previous runs over the distance. On that occasion, I had been on course for a sub three-hour run at fifteen miles when an old injury struck me on the famous or maybe infamous Heartbreak Hill and forced me to walk the rest of the way to the finishing line. While it might have been more prudent to give up on that occasion, I told myself that I hadn't come that far to drop out.

Cork City Marathon - 1984

Heartbreak Hill:
Boston Marathon - 1984

And finally, the publication of my account of the journey to date came to pass in 2013, despite the several times I thought I should press the delete button on the keyboard. My long-suffering wife Mary always managed to intervene, and thanks to her patience, the story survived to be told.

I have been fortunate in my journey through life to have met great people both professionally and socially. I have always been aware of my shortcomings and done my best to surround myself with the greatest of people who have stood by me in the many projects and ventures I have undertaken over the years. There were many times when journeys seemed all uphill and at times hopeless, so many thanks to those who had the tenacity to bear with me when they would have been well justified in giving up on me. I learned that it is always important to surround myself, even in retirement, with gifted people who inspire me towards what President Michael D. Higgins referred to in his 2011 Christmas message as "crafting many great possibilities yet to be imagined". Life on the sports field taught me a few lessons in survival that have served me well in both my professional and personal life. I learned the value of thinking ahead, especially when the going gets tough - never give an adversary a second chance and keep them guessing always.

Whenever people ask me about my bucket list, my reply is simple; getting my legs on the floor in the morning and embracing the day. Every day is a good day now. Recessions and bad times will come and go - have a rant and get over it because it is important to remain focused on the good things in life. Remain loyal to your values, be grateful for family and friends. Since I retired, breakfast has become a banquet with no fixed time limits. Catching up with breaking news online and taking Buddy for a stroll around the neighbourhood is part of my morning ritual now too. I have learned that it is vital to wash and shave before coming downstairs. Otherwise, even Buddy can occasionally object to my hygiene standards.

Life has been quite different for me and my family since I was diagnosed with cancer. Boosted psychologically by the greater periods of time between check-ups now, I am busy living. In fact, I find myself living life in an unrelenting hurry, fuelled by the fear and knowledge that I will run out of time to do the things I need to do. Although I am now only fifty-nine years old, I do realise that I have seen more yesterdays than I have tomorrows left in my life, regardless of what takes me to the end game.

When that time comes, some people will consider me luckier than most. I was diagnosed in 2004 and was gifted so many additional years of life when compared to many other people who were less fortunate and had a much shorter journey with cancer. That will be a fair and rational comment from their perspective. However, I will fight cancer with all that is in me to keep it at bay. I will do what it takes to live life on my terms. Somebody once said that, "You have reached middle age when you have more memories than plans and dreams for the future." If that be the case, let my imagination run wild to feed my plans and dreams.

I have been a dreamer all my life. I have pursued many of them, driven in the pursuit by the rush of adrenalin that comes with the feeling of *"I did it!"* Maybe I have been, and some would suggest that I still am, an adrenalin junkie. And if the cap fits, I'll wear it! The day I stop dreaming will be the day that I cease to be. I must continue to dream and continue to live life in a hurry. There is no point in dwelling on the past and the future will always take care of itself. There are no long-term plans or projects. I am grateful that I am still alive because there were times when the prospects were not encouraging. For now, I enjoy every day as it comes, from sunrise to sunset, in the hope that I will manage to keep the evil enemy called cancer at bay. I have to remain positive and not burden myself, my family and those with whom I interact with the fear and uncertainty that cancer brings. I am always mindful of Ella Wheeler Wilcox's philosophy from the first line of her poem *"Solitude"* (1883), "Laugh, and the world laughs with you; weep, and you weep alone."

Life has taught me many lessons and most important among these is the power of positive thinking and a positive attitude. It has been my experience that opportunity finds those who seek it relentlessly in the mayhem of everyday life. This philosophy taught me to surround myself with great people and I fed from their energy and enthusiasm. Whenever life seemed to be going against me or the struggle was all uphill, my late father's philosophy *"It is better to keep trying than sitting and sighing and waiting the tide"* rang loudest in my ears and drove me on. Consequently, I have learned not to sit around waiting for luck or opportunity to come knocking at the door looking for me. Neither have I sat around crying and complaining about the hand in life that was dealt to me. No. On the contrary, life taught me to take risks, learn from the outcomes, positive or negative, and to do it better next time. Life happens in the fast lane and the older I get, the faster that lane gets. Life is constantly racing ahead; technology and medicine are prime examples of this. Failure to keep up causes us to risk becoming uncoupled like a railroad carriage at the station as the train pulls away. Life is complex and we arrive on this planet without a manual, so we have to grow and adapt to ever-changing circumstances, whether they are social, emotional, economic, physical or whatever. It all happens in a heartbeat.

Life is too short and I feel that time, the subtle thief, bears in with greater speed with every passing day. I am reminded of a line from *One Foot in the Grave* a BBC television sitcom written by David Renwick, when Victor Meldrew, played by Richard Wilson, remarked, "When I was young it seemed as if my birthday only came around every few years, while now it seems to come round every few weeks!" Procrastination was never a way of life that appealed to me, as anyone who knows me will testify. I have never spent time trying to recreate the past because I firmly believe that life moves in one direction; forward. Some might have good reason to suggest that I was impetuous at times and rushed headlong into things when a more cautious approach could and should have been adopted. That is just the way I am and I doubt if I will change any time soon. Whatever might have been the road better chosen, I have no regrets. I was happy to do things as I saw fit, evaluate the outcomes and learn from the experience. In like manner, although I was frightened out of my wits when I was diagnosed with cancer, I do feel that my sense of urgency with regard to having a second sample of bone marrow taken from my pelvis regardless of the discomfort and the follow-up procedures, helped. Now more than ever, I believe in urgency and prioritising, conscious of the reality that is the wisdom of our ancestors when they told us that we are only here *"ar chuaird,"* on a visit.

This account of my journey with cancer was not written as a tale of sickness and woe, or for vain glory or personal gratification. Neither was it written so that my experience might be perceived as a scorch mark or footprint on the literary landscape or because cancer is something that happened to me and me alone. I am not the first person to get cancer and unfortunately, I won't be the last. I am conscious that I am only one person of the twenty-eight million people fighting cancer worldwide every day. We are the cancer community. It is not an exclusive club or one that any of us would have applied to join. However, we are part of it and we need to work together to do what we can to help each other and our families in the war against cancer. This book was written to give hope to people afflicted by cancer and their families who might have to travel a similar route in the awareness that while the going might be tough, the rewards of remission make it all worthwhile. It was also written as a testament of the support I received, and to thank those too numerous to mention who travelled with me and my family in the dark until we arrived at a bright place where all our greatest hopes and dreams came true.

"I am grateful for what I am and have. My thanksgiving is perpetual. It is surprising how contented one can be with nothing definite - only a sense of existence. My breath is sweet to me. O how I laugh when I think of my vague indefinite riches. No run on my bank can drain it, for my wealth is not possession but enjoyment."

-   Henry David Thoreau

The journey with cancer is a route I could never have imagined. Equally, the kindness and support I received was beyond description and I will remain eternally grateful to all of you who travelled with me and now share the journey in this book. I pray you and yours will be safe. I wish you every good health and happiness always.

Kindest regards,

Kevin

Brian & Méabh on their Wedding Day - 16th August 2013.
Photograph courtesy of Cian O'Dwyer

Mary and I with Brian and Méabh on their Wedding Day at St. Joseph's Church, O'Connell Avenue, Limerick - 16th August 2013

Brian and Ronan - August 3013

Acknowledgements

This book would never have come into being if I hadn't been diagnosed with cancer. It is not intended as a personal lament or an attempt to portray myself as a victim of what was, to me, a dreaded disease. Neither is it an exercise in vain glory or an effort to glamorise the attention one attracts when one is diagnosed with cancer.

It is an attempt to acknowledge a journey that started with a routine visit to the doctor and became a journey my family and I could not have envisaged. In so far as it is possible, I wish to acknowledge the support I got from my wife Mary, sons Brian and Ronan, Buddy our dog, my late mother, Annie, extended family, friends, neighbours and the wider community. I would also like to acknowledge the excellent care of a great medical team, namely, our family doctor, Dr. Michael Shinkwin for his early diagnosis, followed by the expert work of Professor R. Gupta and his team in the Cancer Centre in the Mid-West Regional Hospital in Limerick.

I know that people are diagnosed with cancer every day of the year and that somewhere in the region of twenty-eight million people suffer from it worldwide at any given time. Bearing this in mind, I feel it is important to share our experiences so that we can give hope to those who find themselves or their loved ones joining the cancer community at some stage in life.

I decided to share my experience as an ordinary person with non-Hodgkin's follicular lymphoma so that I could provide an insight into my own personal reaction to the ups and downs of the experience, together with the challenges my family had to cope with over the years since diagnosis. Many times, I was reminded of the nursery rhyme about the Grand Old Duke of York and his ten thousand men in that when I was up, I was up and when I was down, I was down, and when I was only half way up, I was neither up nor down!

Equally, my hope is that this book will prove useful to medical teams caring for cancer patients and those in training to work in the cancer care profession. The view from inside my head may afford them some insights into one patient's perspective.

Despite the initial dismal outlook and some significant setbacks along the way, the compass of fortune eventually changed direction to bring some of the greatest moments of relief and happiness to me and all those close to me. It is a personal experience, nothing more and nothing less. I share the journey as a testament to all who travelled with me and enabled me to keep going when it might have been easier to give up. Thankfully, it was the courage, strength and confidence of those who carried me on their backs, and in the process, gave me the strength to look fear in the face, to dig deeper than I ever imagined possible, and to emerge at the other end in one piece. Consequently, my lessons from the experience came more from the journey than its uncertain destination.

My thanks too to **Comhar Linn INTO Credit Union Ltd, Parnell Square, Dublin** for their support. Finally, I want to acknowledge the infinite patience, perseverance and professional expertise of my editor, Trióna Marren O'Grady, without whom this book would never have reached the publisher.